Rocket Science

Also by Jim Wiese

Roller Coaster Science
50 Wet, Wacky, Wild, Dizzy Experiments about Things Kids Like Best

Rocket Science

*50 Flying, Floating, Flipping, Spinning Gadgets
Kids Create Themselves*

Jim Wiese

Illustrations by Tina Cash-Walsh

JOSSEY-BASS
A Wiley Imprint
www.josseybass.com

Published by Jossey-Bass
A Wiley Imprint
989 Market Street, San Francisco, CA 94103-1741   www.josseybass.com

Published simultaneously in Canada.

Illustrations © 1995 by Tina Cash-Walsh.

Jossey-Bass books and products are available through most bookstores. To contact Jossey-Bass directly call our Customer Care Department within the U.S. at 800-956-7739, outside the U.S. at 317-572-3986, or fax 317-572-4002.

Jossey-Bass also publishes its books in a variety of electronic formats. Some content that appears in print may not be available in electronic books.

Library of Congress Cataloging-in-Publication Data

Wiese, Jim.
    Rocket science : 50 flying, floating, flipping, spinning gadgets kids create
themselves / Jim Wiese.
       p.   cm.
    Includes index.
    ISBN 0-471-11357-3 (paper)
    1. Science—Experiments—Juvenile literature. 2. Power (Mechanics)—
Experiments—Juvenile literature. [1. Machinery—Experiments. 2. Science projects.
3. Science—Experiments. 4. Experiments.] I. Title.
Q164.W532 1995
    507.8—dc20   95-2092

For Barbara because of her support and patience,
for Matthew and Elizabeth because of the joy they bring me, and
for my mom and dad because of their inspiration.

Acknowledgments

It would be difficult to name all the people who have helped me in my journey to become a writer of children's science books. However, several people stand out as significant in that they helped point me in the direction that I am now going. Special thanks go to Loren Fickett, who gave me my first teaching job and who saw something in me that I may not have seen myself; Dick Merrill and Pam Rutherford, who urged me to share my science-teaching ideas with others; Doug Pearson, who worked with me to expand my teaching ideas and who never thought that my ideas were crazy; and Gail Wallin and Brian Hansen, who gave me my first writing jobs. Thanks again to John Wiley & Sons, Inc., especially my editor, Kate Bradford, and her assistant editor, Kara Raezer. Their belief in me has made this book possible.

Contents

3 Water, Water Everywhere
Using Water Power to Make Wonderful Inventions   48

4 Don't Be Shocked If You're Attracted to These Activities
Using Electricity and Magnetism to Make Amazing Devices   60

5 Great Chemistry
Using Chemistry to Make Cool Creations   72

6 Strings and Things
Using Acoustics to Build Dynamite Devices   85

7 Lighten Up!
Using Optics to Create Fantastic Fun   96

Introduction

Have you ever wondered how a camera takes pictures? How rockets are launched? Why kites fly or boats float? All of these things can be explained by basic science. In this book you'll construct some wacky inventions that will teach you about the way things work. You'll make Yogurt Cup Phones to understand how sound travels, construct a Paper Plate Flyer to see how objects fly, make a Broomstick Pulley to experiment with mechanics, and create a Lemon Light to learn about electricity. When you make these and dozens of other gadgets, you'll discover that science is a part of every object in our daily lives. Who knows? Maybe someday you'll invent your own fascinating machines and gadgets—or even grow up to be a rocket scientist!

How to Use This Book

This book is divided into chapters based on the general subjects of mechanics, air power, water power, electricity and magnetism, chemistry, acoustics, and optics. In each chapter there are groups of projects that teach you about a specific scientific idea within the general subject. Each project has a list of materials and a procedure to follow. You'll be able to find most of the necessary materials around the house or at your neighborhood hardware, electronics, or grocery store. Some of the projects have a section called More Fun Stuff to Do that lets you try different variations on the original activity. Explanations are given at the end of each group of projects. Words in **bold** type are defined in text and in the Glossary at the back of the book.

Being a Good Scientist

- Read through the instructions once completely and collect all the equipment you'll need before you start the activity or experiment.

- If possible, keep a notebook. Write down what you do in your experiment or project and what happens.

- Follow the instructions carefully. *Do not attempt to do yourself any steps that require the help of an adult.*

- If your experiment or project does not work properly the first time, try again or try doing it in a slightly different way. In real life, experiments don't always work out perfectly the first time.

- Always have an open mind that asks questions and looks for answers. The basis of good science is asking good questions and finding the best answers.

Increasing Your Understanding

- Make small changes in the design of the equipment or project to see if the results stay the same. Change only one thing at a time so you can tell which change caused a particular result.

- Make up an experiment or activity to test your own ideas about how things work.

- Look at the things around you for examples of the scientific principles that you have learned.

- Don't worry if at first you don't understand the things around you. There are always new things to discover. Remember that many of the most famous discoveries were made by accident.

Using This Book to Do a Science Fair Project

Many of the activities in this book can serve as the starting point for a science fair project. After doing the experiment as it is written in the book, what questions come to mind? Some possible projects are suggested in the More Fun Stuff to Do section of the activities.

To begin your science fair project, first write down the problem you want to study and come up with a hypothesis. A **hypothesis** is an educated guess about the results of an experiment you are going to perform. The purpose of a hypothesis is to give a possible explanation of how something happens in nature. For example, if you enjoyed making Yogurt Cup Phones, you may want to find out if other types of string will work as well. A hypothesis for this experiment could be that Yogurt Cup Phones will work better using nylon fishing line rather than string or thread.

To test your hypothesis, first devise an experiment. In the Yogurt Cup Phones activity, you might try several other types of string, thread, and nylon fishing line, and observe the results. Be sure to keep careful records of your experiment. Next, analyze the data you recorded. In the Yogurt Cup Phones activity, you would determine if you could hear more clearly using the nylon fishing line than when you used the string or thread. Finally, come up with a conclusion that shows how your results prove or disprove your hypothesis.

This process is called the **scientific method**. When following the scientific method, you begin with a hypothesis, test it with an experiment, analyze the results, and draw a conclusion.

A Word of Warning

Some science experiments can be dangerous. *Ask an adult to help you with experiments that call for adult help, such as those that involve matches or flames, hammers, or other dangerous materials.* Don't forget to ask your parents' permission to use household items, and put away your equipment and clean up your work area when you have finished experimenting. Good scientists are careful and avoid accidents.

Mechanically Inclined

Using Mechanics to Make Minimachines

Think about how your life would be different if you didn't have any machines to help you. A **machine** is simply a device that helps you do work more easily. Machines can be as simple as a wheel or as complicated as an automobile, but all machines help you exert a **force** such as a push or pull on an object. **Work** is done when the object on which you are pushing or pulling moves as a result of your push or pull.

For example, if you want to lift a person off the ground, you could try lifting him with your hands or you could use a seesaw, which is a type of machine. If you exert a force on one end of the seesaw, the person on the other end will rise. You're doing work to lift the person, but it's easier when you use a simple machine.

Mechanics is an area of science that looks at machines and how they work. Try the projects in this chapter to learn more about machines and mechanics.

Move the Earth
LEVERS

The **lever** is one of the earliest and simplest machines. It is made up of a rigid board or bar that is supported at a fixed point called a **fulcrum.**

Archimedes, the Greek philosopher and scientist, once said, "Give me a long enough lever and a place to set the fulcrum, and I could move the earth." Well, in these activities we're not going to move the earth, but we are going to learn about levers. And along the way we're going to have a little fun!

Project 1
DESKTOP LEVER

Try the following project to learn how levers work.

Materials

book
thick marking pen
ruler

Procedure

1. Lift the book with your hands to observe its weight. Set the book aside.

2. Put the marking pen on a table.

3. Place the center of the ruler across the center of the pen so that they form a +.

4. Place the book on one end of the ruler. Lift the book by pushing down on the opposite end of the ruler. Observe how much effort it takes to lift the book using the ruler and pen. Is it easier than lifting the book with your hands?

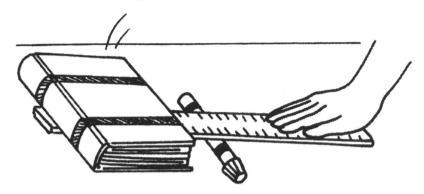

More Fun Stuff to Do ☼

Move the pen to different locations under the ruler and try lifting the book. How can you position the pen so that it is easiest to lift the book?

Project 2 ☼
FLIP GAME

Try the following game to use levers for fun.

Materials

2 spoons
plastic drinking glass

Procedure

1. Place the first spoon faceup on a table. Place the second spoon faceup with its bowl resting on the handle of the first spoon. Place the glass near the handle of the second spoon, as in the diagram.

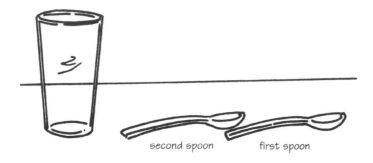

second spoon   first spoon

2. Hit the bowl of the first spoon with your fist. What happens?

3. If you have lined up the spoons and the glass properly, the second spoon will flip into the glass. Can you identify the fulcrum? The lever? The force?

Project 3 ✺
BALANCER

As you know, a seesaw is a type of lever. You may have noticed that if you and a friend sit a certain way on a seesaw, you can balance so that neither of you touches the ground. Sometimes this kind of balance can look very unusual. Try the following activities to see for yourself.

Materials

knife (to be used only
  by an adult)
wooden matchstick
nail
cork

2 identical forks
2 chairs
1-yard (1-m) string
adult helper

Procedure

1. Have an adult use the knife to cut a V-shaped notch in the end of the wooden matchstick. Cut the head off the other end.

2. Use the nail to make a small hole in the middle of the small end of the cork. Insert the head end of the matchstick into the hole so that the notched end points out.

3. Push the forks into the cork on opposite sides, so that they point slightly down.

4. Place the chairs with their backs facing, and tie the string between them. Pull the chairs far enough apart that the string is taut.

5. Place the notched end of the matchstick on the string and balance the lever. What happens?

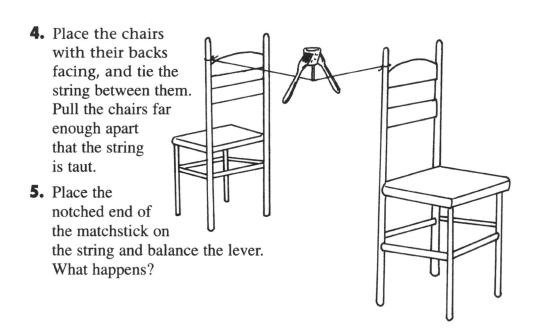

More Fun Stuff to Do ☼

Insert another matchstick between the prongs of the two forks so that the handles of the forks point in opposite directions. Place the match over the mouth of a plastic cup so that the two forks balance and the lever does not dip either way. You may need to experiment with positioning the matchstick and forks to achieve this. Now place the matchstick on the edge of the cup. Adjust the lever so that it balances over the edge.

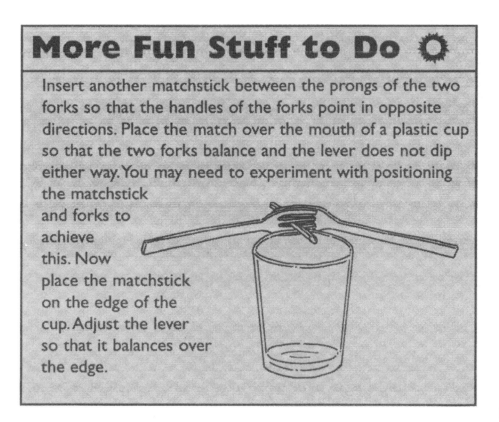

Explanation

A lever is a simple machine. Levers make it easier to lift heavy loads because they magnify the force exerted; in other words, they turn a small force into a big one. You can use a lever to lift a heavy load by setting the load at some place on the lever and positioning the fulcrum in the proper location. The exact force needed to lift the load will depend on the length of the lever and the location of the fulcrum.

The way a lever works is shown in Project 1, Desktop Lever. The ruler is the lever and the marking pen is the fulcrum. The lever and fulcrum allow you to use less force to lift the book than you would use if you lifted the book with your hands. You probably noticed that the closer you move the pen to the book, the less force you need to lift the book.

In Project 2, Flip Game, you use the first spoon as a lever to move the second spoon. The bowl of the first spoon, where it touches the table, acts as a fulcrum, while the handle of the first spoon acts as the lever. When you hit the bowl of the first spoon, that force causes the handle of the spoon to do work, and the second spoon flips into the glass.

Another way to use the lever is shown in Project 3, Balancer. A lever will balance on a fulcrum when all the forces acting on it are centered at or below the fulcrum. In Balancer, the combined **mass**—the amount of material an object contains—of the forks, the cork, and the matchstick acts like one mass placed directly on or, in this case, slightly below the string. Similarly, in More Fun Stuff to Do, the combined mass of the forks and the matchstick acts like one mass placed directly on or slightly below the edge of the glass. With the **center of mass**—the point in an object where its mass is equal in all directions—below the fulcrum, the lever remains in balance because of the stability created. Tightrope walkers in the circus use long poles, often with weights at the ends, to create a similar condition.

Upsy-Daisy
PULLEYS

You might have a hard time lifting a 30-pound (14-kg) weight. If you build a pulley, however, you'll find you can easily lift objects that are too heavy for you to lift on your own.

The **pulley** is a simple machine that can be used to change the amount or direction of a pulling force to make work easier. It is made from a rope or cable that is looped around a support, usually a wheel. The support is often coated with oil or other substances to reduce friction between the rope or cable and the support. **Friction** is a force that stops objects from sliding over each other.

Try the following activities to find out more about friction and pulleys.

Project 1
BROOMSTICK PULLEY

Try the following activity to see pulleys in action.

Materials

2 brooms or other round pieces of wood
rope

talcum powder (optional)
2 helpers

Procedure

1. Ask each of your helpers to hold a broomstick and to stand facing each other about 3 feet (1 m) apart.

2. Tie one end of the rope to one broomstick. Thread the free end of the rope around the other broomstick, then thread it back around the first broomstick. Continue to wind the rope around both broomsticks several times. Hold on to the free end of the rope.

3. If you have talcum powder, spread it on the broomsticks before you give them to your helpers. This will reduce the friction and make it easier for you to pull the brooms together.

4. Ask your helpers to try to pull the brooms apart while you pull on the free end of the rope to try to pull them together. Who is more successful—you or your friends?

Project 2 ☀
SPOOL PULLEY

In this activity, you will make your own pulley to investigate how it works.

Materials

wire cutters or pliers
  (to be used only by an adult)
ruler
wire coat hanger
file (to be used only by an adult)
thread spool
broom

2 chairs
small bucket
several weights (rocks or other
  heavy objects)
about 2 yards (2 m) of heavy
  string
adult helper

Procedure

1. Ask your adult helper to use the wire cutters to cut an 8-inch (20-cm) section from the coat hanger and file down any rough edges.

2. Have the adult bend the wire into a triangular shape so that the ends almost meet in the center of one side of the triangle. Push the ends into the thread spool.

3. Slide the wire triangle over the broomstick and place the broomstick across the seats of 2 chairs.

4. Fill the bucket with weights.

5. Pick up the bucket and observe how much force you need to exert to lift it.

6. Tie one end of the string to the handle of the bucket.

7. Wind the string over the spool to make a pulley, as shown in the diagram.

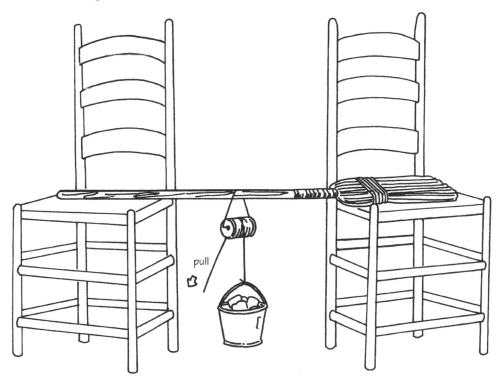

pull

8. Pull down on the other end of the string to lift the bucket. Is it easier to lift the load with this pulley system?

More Fun Stuff to Do

Make a two-pulley system from 2 thread spools, 2 wires, and about 2 yards (2 m) of heavy string. Begin with steps 1 and 2 of the original Procedure, only this time make two triangular wires with thread spools. Before pushing the wire ends into the second spool, slip the bucket with weights over the wire as shown. Slide the other wire triangle over the broomstick that is held up by the two chairs, as in the first Procedure. Tie one end of the string to one of the wires near one end of the lower spool. Thread the string around the spool above and then back around the spool below, then over the upper spool once more.

Pull the string and lift the load. Is it easier to lift the load with this two-pulley system? How much string do you need to pull in order to lift the load 12 inches (30 cm)?

Try making a system that uses several more pulleys. Can you design ways that make it even easier to lift the load? What happens to the amount of string necessary to make your pulley system work better?

Explanation

Like levers, pulleys make it easier to lift a heavy load by magnifying the force you exert to lift the load. Pulleys can also change the direction of the force necessary to lift the load. In Project 1, Broomstick Pulley, you are able to pull the broomsticks together and beat the power of the two people who are trying to pull them apart. The pulley system magnifies your pulling force, making your force greater than that of your helpers.

In Project 2, Spool Pulleys, the first pulley system changes the direction of the force, which allows you to use gravity to help you lift the bucket. **Gravity**—the force that pulls objects toward the earth—pulls on your body as you pull on the rope.

The pulley system in the More Fun Stuff to Do section of Project 2 magnifies your force, but at a cost. To pull with less force, you must pull farther, that is, use more string. You pull with less force for a greater distance. The result is that you do the same amount of work, but it feels easier.

Boing!
ELASTIC ENERGY

Energy is the ability to do work. There are two main types of energy. **Kinetic energy** is the energy of moving objects. **Potential energy** is stored energy that has the ability to change into kinetic energy. Energy is never used up; it is just converted from one form to another.

One kind of potential energy is **elastic energy**. Elastic energy is the energy stored in a material when its shape is changed by either **stretching** (pulling apart) or **compressing** (pushing together). A stretched rubber band and a coiled spring both have stored elastic energy. Stored elastic energy is released when an object is allowed to return to its natural shape. For example, you release energy by shooting a rubber band across the room or letting go of a coiled spring.

Try the following activities to see what you can do using elastic energy.

Project 1
RUBBER-BAND WALKER

Many years ago, someone figured out how to make a thread spool crawl across the room by winding up a rubber band inside it. Try the following project for yourself.

Materials

rubber band about the same
   length as the spool
thread spool
thumbtack

metal washer
matchstick, toothpick, or similar
   object

Procedure

1. Slip the rubber band through the hole in the thread spool so that it passes through the spool from one end to the other.

2. Attach one end of the rubber band to one end of the spool with the thumbtack.

3. Slip the other end of the rubber band through the hole in a metal washer.

4. Put the matchstick through the loop in the rubber band that sticks out through the hole in the washer.

5. Turn the matchstick to wind up the rubber band inside the spool.

6. Place the spool on a table or floor and let it go. What happens?

More Fun Stuff to Do

Try different-sized spools and rubber bands on your walkers. Do they make the walker go faster or farther? Try other materials instead of the metal washer. Will a plastic washer work?

Project 2

ROLL-BACK CAN

This can will return to you when you call. Only it isn't really obeying you; it's obeying the laws of science!

Materials

hammer (to be used
   only by an adult)
2 nails
coffee can with plastic lid
rubber band slightly longer
   than the coffee can

transparent tape
several weights (heavy nuts and
   bolts)
3-inch (7.5-cm) piece of string
adult helper

Procedure

1. Ask an adult to use the hammer and one of the nails to punch a hole in the center of the bottom of the coffee can and a similar hole in the plastic lid.

2. Slip the rubber band through the hole in the bottom of the can— just enough so that a loop pops out of the bottom. Put the nail through the loop, and secure the nail to the outside of the can with tape.

3. Secure weights to the middle of the rubber band midway between the bottom of the can and the lid by tying the string tightly around both the weights and the rubber band.

4. Pull the free end of the rubber band through the hole in the plastic lid. The rubber band should be taut. Slip the other nail through the loop in the rubber band, and secure the nail to the lid with tape. Snap the lid onto the can.

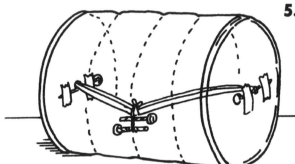

5. Gently roll the can on a hard, smooth, level surface. Just before the can stops rolling, command it to return. The can will obey! Can you guess why?

Project 3 ☀
MOUSETRAP CAR

Releasing a rubber band isn't the only way to capture the power of elastic energy. Another way is to use a coiled spring, such as the spring in a standard mousetrap. Try the following activity and see how to use the elastic energy of a spring to build a self-powered car.

Materials

pencil
cardboard
small drinking glass or jar lid
scissors
glue
4 corks
nail
wire cutters or pliers (to be
   used only by an adult)

wire coat hanger
file (to be used only by an adult)
2 plastic drinking straws
transparent tape
mousetrap
8-inch (20-cm) piece of string
stick
adult helper

Procedure

1. Draw four 2-inch (5-cm) circles on the cardboard. This can be simplified by tracing around a small glass or jar lid. Cut them out with the scissors. These are the wheels of the car.

2. Glue a cork to the center of each of the four wheels. The larger end of the cork should be attached to each wheel. Make a hole in the center of each cork with the nail.

3. Have an adult use the wire cutters to cut two 4-inch (10-cm) pieces of wire from the coat hanger, then file down any rough edges.

4. Cut two 3½-inch (8-cm) pieces of straw. Slip a piece of straw onto each wire.

5. Put glue on the ends of the wire and insert them into the holes in the four corks. The corks, wires, and straws are the two axles of your car.

6. Tape or glue the straws to the bottom of the mousetrap about 3 inches (7.5 cm) apart. Wrap one end of the string around one of the corks of the rear axle. Tie the other end of the string to the wire snapper of the mousetrap so that it is taut.

7. Pull the wire snapper and set it into place according to the mousetrap instructions.

8. Place the mousetrap car on the floor.

CAUTION: A mousetrap can hurt you if it snaps your fingers. Be very careful when you set your mousetrap!

9. Use the stick to "trip" the mousetrap, and watch your car go! Which type of elastic energy is your car using?

More Fun Stuff to Do ☼

There is no "right" way to build a mousetrap car. Experiment with materials that you have around the house. Keep what works and discard what doesn't. Try jar lids, checkers, or thread spools for wheels. Try using wheels of different sizes. Does it make a difference if the wheels in the front are bigger or smaller than the wheels in the back? Use different materials to build the axles. Remember, anything goes, as long as the car goes!

Explanation

Elastic energy, the potential energy stored in a material when its shape is changed, is useful when it is converted into other forms of energy. In the previous activities, elastic energy is stored in either a stretched rubber band or a coiled spring. The gadgets that you built convert that stored energy into a more useful form of energy called kinetic energy, the energy of moving objects.

In Project 1, Rubber-Band Walker, and Project 3, Mousetrap Car, stored elastic energy is converted directly to kinetic energy. You wind up the rubber band inside the walker and set the spring inside the mousetrap to store the elastic energy. When you release the rubber band and spring the mousetrap, elastic energy is converted to kinetic energy and the walker and car move.

In Project 2, Roll-Back Can, the forward movement of the can winds the rubber band, and kinetic energy is converted to stored elastic energy. When the kinetic energy given to the can by your push is used up, the can stops rolling. The stored energy in the rubber band then causes it to unwind. The elastic energy is converted back to kinetic energy, and the can rolls back to you.

You've Got the Power

Using Air Power to Make Great Gadgets

The **air** that surrounds us is a gas. Gases and liquids are considered **fluids**, meaning that they flow and can change their shape easily. Air contains small particles called **molecules** that move around freely, allowing air to change shape to fit a certain space. This movement of air molecules creates a constant pressure called **air pressure**.

We cannot see the air, yet we know it is there because of what it does. We depend on the oxygen in the air to breathe. We feel the wind on our bodies and see it blowing through the trees. The power of gases and moving air can even lift a rocket to the moon and beyond!

Try the projects in this section to see the many ways you can use the power of air.

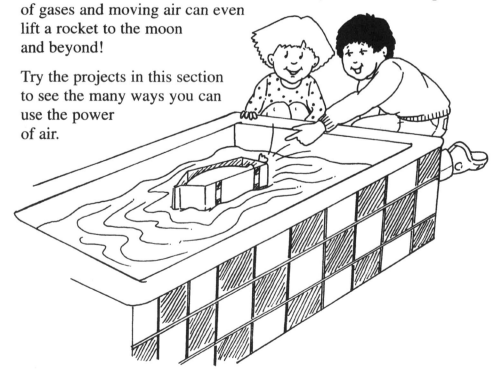

Blast Off!
BALLOON ROCKETS

On July 20, 1969, after years of planning, research, and experimentation, astronaut Neil Armstrong became the first person to set foot on the moon. But the human fascination with space travel has existed for centuries. Space-traveling objects began with the first rockets built by the Chinese in the twelfth century, progressed to the space shuttles that fly today, and will continue with the future designs of tomorrow. These flying devices all operate using the same basic scientific principles. Try the following activities and projects, and who knows, maybe someday you'll help design the space vehicles that will take us beyond our solar system.

Project 1
ROCKET BOAT

Next time you go to the lake or even take a bath, take a rocket boat with you and see what you can learn.

Materials

scissors
1-quart (1-liter) cardboard milk carton (empty and clean)
balloon
bathtub, sink, or any body of still water

Procedure

1. Cut one side off the milk carton as shown. With scissors, make a hole approximately ½ inch (1.25 cm) in diameter in the bottom of the carton.

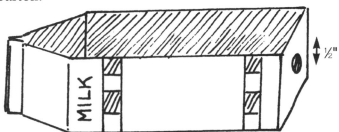

2. Blow up the balloon, and pinch the end closed. Do not make a knot. Place the balloon in the milk carton boat, and slip the end through the hole in the bottom of the carton, being careful not to let the air out of the balloon.

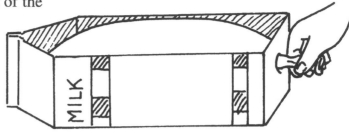

3. Place the boat in the water, and release the end of the balloon. What happens to the boat?

More Fun Stuff to Do

Repeat the experiment with a ½-gallon (2-liter) milk carton. Try using different-sized balloons. Experiment with putting weight in the boat using plasticine (modeling clay) or other weights. What is the best design to make the boat go the farthest?

Project 2 ☼
HORIZONTAL ROCKET

Now that you've mastered making boats, try making a rocket.

Materials

oblong balloon
10-foot (3-m) string or nylon
   fishing line
drinking straw

2 chairs
transparent tape
scissors

Procedure

1. Blow up the balloon, and tie the end in a knot.

2. Thread the string through the straw.

3. Tie the ends of the string to the chairs. The straw should move freely along the string.

4. Tape the balloon to the straw as shown. Slide the balloon so the knotted end is next to one of the chairs. What happens to the balloon?

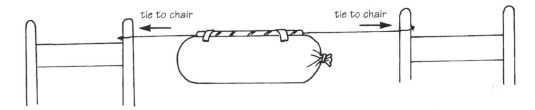

tie to chair   tie to chair

5. Leaving the balloon in place next to the chair, cut off the knotted end of the balloon with scissors. What happens this time?

More Fun Stuff to Do ☼

Repeat the experiment using a different-sized balloon, or try blowing up the balloon with more or less air. Experiment with other ways to make the balloon rocket move faster or farther. Using construction paper, make fins or a nose cone for your rocket. Insert a straw or a rolled piece of paper in the end of the balloon instead of tying the end. Does the size of the opening made with straw or paper have an effect on the performance of the rocket? If so, how?

Project 3 ✺
VERTICAL ROCKET

Once you have mastered the horizontal rocket, try to launch one vertically.

Materials

2 oblong balloons
scissors
string or nylon fishing line
2 drinking straws
transparent tape

Styrofoam cup
weights (such as nuts, bolts, or
    clay)
adult helper

Procedure

Part 1

1. Blow up one of the balloons, and tie the end in a knot.

2. Cut a piece of string that is a little longer than the distance from the floor to the ceiling.

3. Thread the string through one of the straws.

4. Ask an adult to tape one end of the string to the ceiling. Tape the other end to the floor.

5. Tape the balloon to the straw as shown, with the knot facing the floor. Slide the balloon so the knotted end is almost touching the floor. What happens to the balloon?

6. Leave the balloon in place near the floor. Cut off the knotted end of the balloon with scissors. What happens this time?

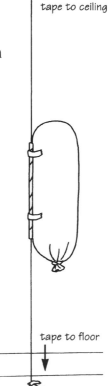

tape to ceiling

tape to floor

Part 2

1. Repeat steps 1 through 5 from Part 1 with the second balloon.

2. Cut three 12-inch (30-cm) pieces of string.

3. Tape one end of each string to the Styrofoam cup. Tape the other ends of the strings to the knotted end of the balloon so that the cup is suspended underneath it.

4. Cut the knotted end of the balloon with the scissors. What happens? Is the balloon rocket capable of carrying the cup up with it?

5. Repeat the experiment, but this time add some of the weights to the cup. Can the rocket lift off with this extra weight? How much weight can the balloon lift?

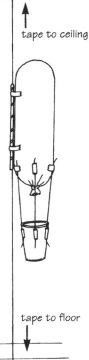

tape to ceiling

tape to floor

More Fun Stuff to Do ✸

Try both experiments again using different-sized balloons, or try blowing up the balloons with more or less air. Experiment with other ways to make the balloon rockets move faster or farther. Design your balloon rockets to lift the most weight possible.

Project 4 ☼
TWO-STAGE ROCKET

Now that you have mastered a simple rocket, it's time to move on to a more advanced one.

Materials

scissors
drinking straw
20-foot (6-m) string or nylon
   fishing line
2 chairs

3- or 4-ounce (90- or 120- ml)
   paper cup
2 oblong balloons
transparent tape
helper

Procedure

NOTE: If you do not have a long hallway, this activity can be done outdoors.

1. Cut the straw into four equal pieces. Place the four pieces of straw on the string, and tie the ends of the string between the chairs.

2. Cut out the bottom of the paper cup. Slide the top of the cup over the first balloon (balloon A) so that the open end of the balloon sticks out through the open bottom of the cup. Stretch the balloon and blow it up.

3. Pinch the balloon closed, then bend the pinched end over the open bottom of the cup and hold it there.

4. Have your helper insert the second balloon (balloon B) in the open bottom of the cup and blow the balloon up. When the balloon is inflated, the cup should fit snugly around the balloon. Your helper should pinch the end of balloon B closed but not make a knot. You should now be able to release the pinched end of balloon A. The inflated balloon B should hold balloon A closed.

5. Have your helper continue to pinch balloon B closed and hold the balloon-cup-balloon contraption together while you tape it to the four pieces of straw as shown in the diagram.

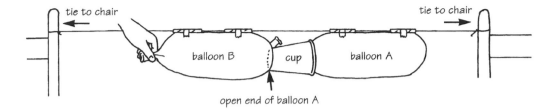

tie to chair

tie to chair

balloon B

cup

balloon A

open end of balloon A

6. Have your helper release balloon B. What happens?

More Fun Stuff to Do ☼

Repeat the experiment with balloons of different sizes and shapes. Try to make a two-stage rocket that will go the farthest or the fastest.

Explanation

All of the projects in this section work because of **Newton's three laws of motion**:

1. An object at rest will stay at rest and an object in motion will stay in motion, unless they are acted upon by an outside force.

2. An object will move with an **acceleration**—increasing speed—that is proportional to the force applied to it.

3. For every action, there is an equal and opposite reaction.

In all of the experiments, the balloon does not move at first because of Newton's first law. There is no force acting on the balloon, so it stays still.

However, the air inside the balloon is under pressure. When the knotted end is cut or the pinched end is let go, the pressurized air inside the balloon escapes, creating a force. The air rushing out of the balloon creates an action force in one direction. The reaction force, according to Newton's third law, is equal and in the opposite direction. It is the reaction force that causes the balloon to move along the string. The more you blow a balloon up, the more force you create and the faster the balloon should go (Newton's second law).

In Project 4, Two-Stage Rocket, balloon B pushed balloon A to start. As balloon B deflated, it released balloon A, which released its air and kept moving.

In all of these projects, the balloons eventually stop moving. If an object stops, then according to Newton's first law, it must have a force acting on it. Friction between the straw and the string, air resistance against the balloon, and weights in the Styrofoam cup are forces that act against the movement of the balloon.

Without the opposing forces caused by friction, the balloon rockets would keep going. This is what occurs in outer space, where there is little resistance from the air. A space rocket will give a big blast from its engine to escape the earth's gravity. After that initial blast, the rocket mainly coasts to its destination, even if the trip takes several years.

Air Energy
WINDMILLS

There are other ways, besides rockets, to use the power of air. Wind has been used for many years to do work. In the seventh century, Persians harnessed the power of wind in a windmill. Early wind-mills used moving air to turn blades that rotated grindstones inside a mill. These grindstones ground various grains such as wheat and corn into flour for baking.

Recently, scientists have returned to using the power of the wind to create electricity. So you see, air power can be used to make elec-tricity, to fly, or just to have fun. The activities in this section use air and its power to fuel fantastic gadgets.

Project 1
ROTOR

There are several simple windmills that you can make. One of the easiest to build is a rotor. A **rotor** is the part that moves in a motor.

Materials

scissors
1-foot (30-cm) -long cardboard tube
   (such as the tube inside a roll of
   paper towels or plastic wrap)
transparent tape or glue
wire cutters or pliers (to be used only
   by an adult)

wire coat hanger
file (to be used only by
   an adult)
2 empty thread spools
adult helper

Procedure

1. Carefully cut the cardboard tube in half lengthwise.

2. Tape or glue together one edge of the two halves of the tube so the curved parts face in opposite directions as shown. This is the rotor.

3. Have an adult cut and straighten a coat hanger to make a piece of wire about 18 inches (45 cm) long, then file down any rough edges. This is the axle for the rotor.

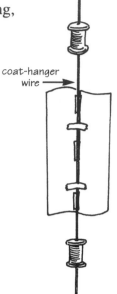

coat-hanger wire →

4. Tape or glue the axle along the center of the rotor where the halves of the tube are connected.

5. Slide an empty thread spool on each end of the axle to use as the handles.

6. Blow on the rotor. What happens? What happens when you place it in a breeze?

Project 2 ☼
WINDMILL

Experimental windmills, designed to produce electricity for homes and businesses, have been built in many areas of the world. Try building the next gadget, and see if you can produce enough energy to lift a small weight.

Materials

scissors
plastic lid from a coffee can
3-inch (7.5-cm) nail
glue

1-inch (2.5-cm) piece of plastic
   drinking straw
1-foot (30-cm) piece of string
bolt

Procedure

1. Cut the plastic coffee-can lid into the shape of propeller blades as shown. Make a small hole in the center with a nail.

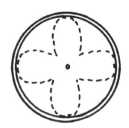

2. Push the nail through the hole so that the head of the nail fits against the lid. Glue the nail in place.

3. After the glue has dried, gently twist one edge of each blade of the propeller toward you in the same lengthwise direction so the blades can catch the wind. Always bend the same edge on each blade. This is your windmill.

4. Slide the piece of straw onto the nail. Hold your windmill in front of you by grasping the straw. Blow on your windmill blades. The blades should turn. If they do not, bend the blades a little bit more.

5. Tie one end of the string to the bolt. Tie the other end of the string to the nail, near its pointed end.

6. Hold the straw and blow on the blades. Can you create enough energy to wind the string around the nail and lift the bolt?

More Fun Stuff to Do ☼

See if you can create windmills using other materials. Make a larger windmill using cardboard instead of a plastic lid. Can a larger windmill lift larger loads?

Explanation

A windmill is a machine that uses kinetic energy—the energy of moving objects—to do work. The kinetic energy of moving air turns the propeller blades of your windmill. The blades turn the nail, and the turning motion of the nail lifts the bolt. If a windmill is attached to a machine called an electric **generator**, the kinetic energy of the wind is converted to electricity, another form of energy. Windmills have been used to do all kinds of work, from grinding grains to pumping water to generating electricity for homes and businesses.

Smooth Sailing
SAILBOATS

Have you ever watched a sailboat as it glides over the water? Did you wonder how it can sail in almost any direction, even though the wind moves only one way? Try the following project and you'll be on course for smooth sailing!

Project
SAILBOAT

Try building your own sailboat and see if you can discover how it harnesses the wind.

Materials

small matchbox or 4-inch (10-cm) -square piece of aluminum foil
scissors
heavy paper (such as construction paper)

transparent tape
toothpick or small stick
plasticine (modeling clay)
bathtub, sink, or any body of still water

Procedure

1. Use the inside of the matchbox for the body of your boat, or fold the aluminum foil into the shape of a boat.

2. Cut a triangular sail, about 3 inches (8 cm) long on one side, from the paper. Tape the sail to the toothpick, then attach one end of the toothpick to the body of the boat with plasticine.

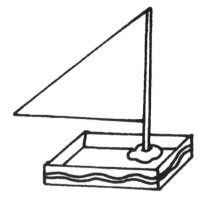

3. Float the boat in the water. You may have to reposition the sail to get the boat to float properly.

4. Blow on the sail and watch what happens. What happens when you blow on the sail from different directions?

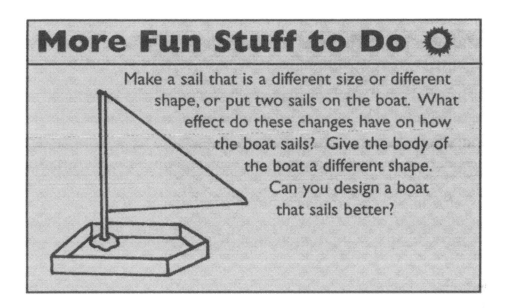

More Fun Stuff to Do ☼

Make a sail that is a different size or different shape, or put two sails on the boat. What effect do these changes have on how the boat sails? Give the body of the boat a different shape. Can you design a boat that sails better?

Explanation

The direction that a sailboat travels depends on both the direction that the wind is blowing and the direction that the boat is steered. The wind pushes the boat's sail in one direction, while the boat's steering uses the water to exert a force in the same or a different direction. The combination of these two forces determines the direction that the boat travels through the water.

A boat that is not steered, such as the sailboat you made, travels in a direction that depends only on the wind. The wind's effect can be controlled by changing the design of the sail. The shape of the sail, the number of sails, and the location of the sails on the boat all affect how a sailboat travels, as each variation catches the wind differently.

New sailboat designs are tried every year as people try to make their sailboats move faster through the water. The shape of sails has changed as well. Some sails are even shaped like airplane wings!

Take Off!
PLANES, KITES, AND FLIGHT

Have you ever wondered what makes an airplane fly? Planes and other flying objects use the wind indirectly through **Bernoulli's principle**. Daniel Bernoulli was a Swiss scientist who discovered that when any fluid, such as air, flows, its pressure decreases as its speed increases. This decrease in air pressure can lift objects from a Frisbee to a jet airplane!

Project 1 ☼
PAPER PLANE

Different paper planes fly differently because of their shape or function. Some are long and thin, designed for long, straight flights. Others have large wing areas for slow, looping flights and for performing stunts. Build this paper plane, and then modify it to make it fly better.

Materials

8½-by-11-inch (22-by-28-cm) sheet of paper

Procedure

1. Fold the paper in half lengthwise. Unfold it.

2. Bend the paper in half widthwise to find the center. Pinch the paper at the center, but do not make a complete crease. Unfold it. Fold the paper so that the left end meets the center. The folded section should be one-fourth the width of the paper.

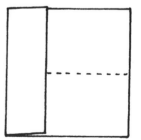

3. Fold the folded section in half again to find the center. Unfold it. Fold in the two left corners so that they meet in the center of the folded section.

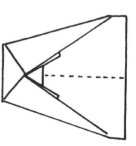

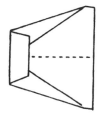

4. Fold the folded section in half.

5. Fold the paper in half along the original lengthwise crease, but fold in the opposite direction as shown. The folded sections made in steps 2 through 4 should still be visible.

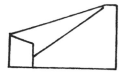

6. Make the wings by making a fold in each half of the plane parallel to the original fold. Now fly your paper plane!

More Fun Stuff to Do ☼

There are many modifications that you can make to a paper plane if you want it to fly differently. Try these ways to modify your paper plane design to make it fly better.

1. Add lift to the wings or fins by folding the forward (front) edge of the wings down slightly toward the bottom of the plane. This is an ideal fold if you want to make gliders loop.

2. Create tail lift. If your plane dives, gently curl the tail end of the wings upward. This will give the plane more lift. If your plane veers left or right, try curling the side of the tail opposite to the direction the plane veered.

3. Seal the body of the plane. This method is used by many professional paper-plane enthusiasts who enter their models in competition. If the open part of the body of the plane (the fuselage) is sealed with tape or glue, the result is greater speed and agility.

When you experiment with your plane, always make sure the paper plane is symmetrical. One common problem with paper planes is that their left and right halves are not exactly the same. Be very careful when you make the paper plane that both sides are the same.

Project 2 ☀
PAPER-PLATE FLYER

You've probably played with a Frisbee before, but have you ever tried to make one for yourself? Although the science behind why they fly is not entirely known, we do know how to make them and how to have fun!

Materials

large paper plate
Play-Doh or plasticine (modeling clay)

Procedure

1. Turn the paper plate upside down, and try to fly it like a Frisbee. What happens?

2. Place a small amount of Play-Doh in several places around the outside edge of the plate to give it weight. Distribute the weight as evenly as possible.

3. Give your redesigned plate a backhand toss and see how it flies. Does it fly better with the weights than without?

More Fun Stuff to Do ☀

Try different types of paper plates and different amounts and types of weight to see if you can improve on the Frisbee design.

Project 3 ☀

SLED KITE

People have long been fascinated by flight and have always wanted to fly. Kites marked the beginning of our quest to overcome the earth's gravity. Build a special kite called a sled kite and experience the fascination firsthand.

Materials

plastic garbage bag at least
   24 × 30 inches (60 × 75 cm)
scissors
yardstick (meterstick)
marking pen

roll of duct tape or packing tape
2 wooden dowels 24 inches
   (60 cm) long and ⅛ inch
   (3 mm) in diameter
string

Procedure

1. Flatten the plastic garbage bag on a large tabletop, and cut out a 24-by-30-inch (60-by-75-cm) rectangle.

2. On each long edge of the rectangle, make a mark 6 inches (15 cm) from each corner.

3. On two short edges, make a mark 8 inches (20 cm) from each corner as shown. Use the yardstick (meterstick) to connect the marks on each edge with the marking pen as shown.

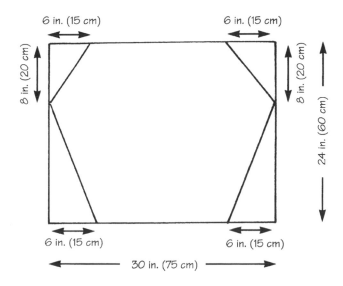

4. Cut along the lines made by the marking pen.

5. Place a small piece of duct tape faceup each of the four points where you made a 6-inch (15-cm) mark. Place the tape so that half of it is stuck to the plastic and the other half is free.

6. Place each dowel between two opposite points as shown, and fold the tape over to secure the dowels to the plastic.

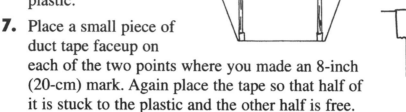

7. Place a small piece of duct tape faceup on each of the two points where you made an 8-inch (20-cm) mark. Again place the tape so that half of it is stuck to the plastic and the other half is free.

8. Cut a piece of string 2 yards (2 m) long. Place the ends of the string on each piece of exposed tape with enough string left over so that you can later tie it in a knot. Fold the tape over the string to secure it to the plastic.

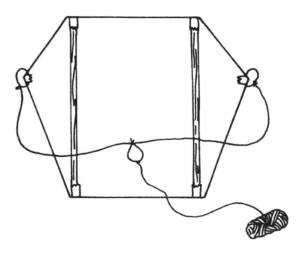

9. Lift the kite by the string to determine the center of the string. If you fold the kite exactly in half, this should be easy. Tie a loop knot in the center of the string.

10. Tie the end of the remaining string to the loop knot. Now fly your kite!

Try making a kite out of newspaper or other material. How does it work compared to the plastic kite? Can you design a kite that will fly better?

Explanation

The projects in this section use the power of air to fly. When any fluid, like air, flows, its pressure decreases as its speed increases. This is called Bernoulli's principle, and it helps explain why planes and other objects fly.

In Project 1, Paper Plane, when the plane's wing moves through the air, some of the air goes above the wing and some of the air goes below the wing. The wing of the plane is shaped so that it is slightly larger on the top surface than on the bottom surface. This shape makes the air moving on the top surface flow slightly faster, which causes a decrease in air pressure above the wing. This decrease in pressure creates lift on the wing, which is what makes the plane fly.

As the paper-plate flyer in Project 2 moves through the air, the air is forced over the top of the inverted plate. This air increases the plate's speed and decreases its pressure. This decrease in pressure creates a low-pressure area above the plate, and the plate is lifted into the air. The extra weight added to the outer edge of the plate increases the stability of the plate as it spins. The spin creates a **gyroscopic effect**, meaning that a rotating object has a more stable flight than an object that doesn't spin. The combination of the gyroscopic effect and the lift in the paper-plate flyer and in Frisbees results in a stable flight.

The flight of the kite in Project 3, Sled Kite, can also be explained by Bernoulli's principle. The wind blowing over the kite results in a decrease in air pressure above the kite, causing the kite to be lifted into the air. Like the paper-plate flyer, the sled kite has a special design that makes it very stable in flight. The two wooden dowels along each side and the long bridle—the string that attaches one side of the kite to the other—expose a large area of the kite to the wind. This design allows the kite to remain in an upright position and to fly in very light wind.

Under Pressure
AIR PRESSURE INVENTIONS

So far, you've used the power of air for rockets, windmills, sail-boats, and some flying devices. You've just begun to see what air can do. Air pressure can be useful as well.

Air pressure pushes down on us all the time, but because it pushes down on all sides of us, we don't feel it. Try the following projects using air pressure to learn more.

Project 1
AIR PUMP

Air exists all around us. Although you can't see it, it occupies space, has weight, and exerts pressure. Try the following activity to investigate air pressure and the force that it creates.

Materials

scissors
6 or 7 drinking straws
small plastic bag (such as a freezer
   or produce bag) approximately
   9 × 12 inches (13.5 × 30 cm)

transparent tape
several heavy books
large plastic trash bag
5 or 6 helpers

Procedure

Part 1

1. Cut one end of a straw at an angle so that it makes a point that can be poked through a plastic bag.

2. Flatten the small plastic bag to remove the air. Tape the end closed so that no air can enter.

3. Insert the pointed end of the straw into the bag near one of the outer edges, leaving most of the straw outside the bag. Tape the straw to the bag so that there are *no air leaks*.

4. Place several heavy books on top of the bag.

5. Blow through the straw and try to lift the books. What happens?

Part 2

1. Make a point in the remaining straws, and give one to each helper.

2. Spread the large plastic bag on the floor.

3. Flatten the bag to remove the air. Tape the end closed so that no air can enter.

4. Ask one helper to volunteer to be lifted by air alone. The others will cause the lift.

5. Have the other helpers insert their straws into the bag near the outer edges, leaving most of the length of each straw outside the bag. Tape the straws to the bag so that there are *no air leaks*.

6. Have the volunteer sit on the bag while the others blow through their straws. What happens?

More Fun Stuff to Do ☼

If the volunteer lies down on the bag, will it be easier to lift him or her? What happens if the volunteer stands up? Give everyone a chance to be lifted.

Project 2 ☀

CAN CRUSHER

The air around you has tremendous power. It's pushing on you now, even if you can't detect it. Try the following activity to see the power of air.

Materials

pie pan   empty soda can
tap water   tongs
stove or hot plate (to be used   adult helper
    only by an adult)

NOTE: Procedure requires a stove or hot plate and adult supervision.

Procedure

1. Fill the pie pan with about 1 inch (2.5 cm) of water. Place the pie pan on the counter next to the stove.

2. Place a small amount of water in the empty soda can—just enough to cover the bottom of the can.

3. Have an adult place the soda can with water on a stove burner or hot plate. Let the water boil vigorously for 1 minute. Steam should come out of the can. Turn off the heat.

4. Have an adult use the tongs to quickly turn the can upside down into the pie pan. What happens to the can?

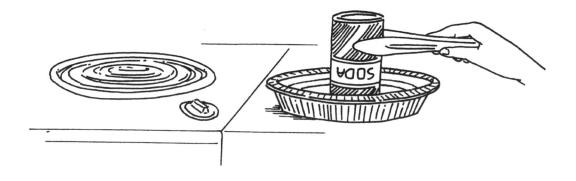

Explanation

Both of the air pump activities in Project 1 use air pressure in the same way. When you blow into the bags, the air molecules in the bags are compressed, or pushed closer together. This compressed air exerts pressure upon the things you are lifting, either the books or your helper, and causes them to rise. When a fluid, either gas or liquid, in a closed container is squeezed by a force, the force is transmitted equally to all parts of the fluid. This is called **Pascal's principle**, the same principle used when you pump up a bicycle tire or inflate a basketball.

The Can Crusher in Project 2 works because of a change in air pressure. You create low air pressure first, then you use the higher pressure outside the can to crush it.

Before it is heated, the can is filled with water and air. When the water is boiled, it **evaporates**—changes from a liquid to a gas. The steam pushes the air out of the can. When the can is turned upside down in the water, the air cannot go back inside the can.

As the water in the pie pan cools, the steam remaining in the can also cools, causing the steam to **condense**—change from gas to a liquid (water). The steam that earlier took up the space inside the can now condenses into a few drops of water, which take up much less space. This causes the air pressure inside the can to drop. The air pressure outside the can is therefore greater, and it pushes on the can, causing the can to collapse.

Hot Air
MORE MOVING WITH BALLOONS

Have you ever watched hot-air balloons gracefully drift overhead? They seem suspended in midair, carried softly by the passing breeze. Occasionally you can hear the roar of the flame they use to float in the air. What makes them rise? Why don't they fall? This unit will help you investigate the mysteries of hot-air balloons.

Project
HOT-AIR BALLOON

How do hot-air balloons float so easily? Build your own hot-air balloon and learn what makes them fly.

Materials

rubber cement	blow-dryer (to be used only by
plastic dry-cleaning bag	an adult)
or other thin plastic bag	2 large books or other heavy objects
paper clips	adult helper

NOTE: Procedure requires a blow-dryer and adult supervision.

Procedure

1. Use rubber cement to seal any small holes in the top of the dry-cleaning bag. This will leave only the large opening at the bottom.

2. Attach several paper clips to the bottom edge of the bag.

3. Without turning the blow-dryer on, position it on the floor between the books. The exhaust end of the dryer (the end the hot air comes out of) should point straight up. Be careful not to block the air intake fan on the side of the dryer.

4. Have an adult set the dryer to its hottest setting and turn it on.

5. Open the bag and hold it over the dryer as shown to fill the bag with hot air. Be careful not to put your hand directly over the exhaust end of the dryer. Hot air can burn your skin. When the bag is completely filled, let it go. What happens?

More Fun Stuff to Do ☼

Repeat the experiment using different types and sizes of plastic bags to see if they fly better. Do lower settings on the blow-dryer work as well?

Explanation

As the air in the plastic bag is heated, the air molecules move faster and farther apart. This causes the air in the bag to become lighter. The lighter air naturally rises, and the bag lifts off. Once the bag has risen and moved away from the source of heat, the air in the bag cools and again becomes heavier. When the weight of the air inside the bag is equal to the weight of the surrounding air, gravity takes over and the bag returns to earth.

Instead of a blow-dryer, real hot-air balloons are fueled by fire. The flame of the fire is increased to allow the balloon to rise and float in the air, and decreased in order for the balloon to land.

47

Water, Water Everywhere

Using Water Power to Make Wonderful Inventions

Water, or H_2O, is made of two parts of hydrogen and one part of oxygen. We find water in a solid form (ice and snow), a liquid form (drinking water, rain, and ocean water), and a gas form (steam). The average human body is 65 percent water by weight, and water covers 70 percent of the surface of the earth.

We often take water for granted. We usually have it in a plentiful supply. We drink it, cook with it, water our lawns and gardens with it, and complain about it during droughts and floods. But water has other uses as well. It can power a rocket, tell time, and even generate electricity. Do you find that hard to believe? Try the following projects and see what water can do.

Blast Off!
WATER ROCKETS

There are many ways to make a rocket fly into space. You have already used air power to launch the balloon rockets in Chapter 2. Chemical reactions, which you will learn more about in Chapter 5, fuel the large rockets that launch humans into space. Rockets can also be launched using high **water pressure**—the force exerted by water that has been compressed.

Project
WATER ROCKET

The following activity uses water to fuel a rocket.

Materials

needle used to inflate basketballs
cork to fit in ½-gallon (2-liter)
  soda bottle
bicycle pump
½-gallon (2-liter) plastic soda
  bottle (empty and clean)

tap water
large **outdoor** area to launch
  rocket
adult helper

NOTE: Procedure must be performed outdoors with adult supervision.

Procedure

1. Ask an adult to insert the needle through the larger end of the cork until the needle opening is visible on the other side of the cork. Then attach the needle to the bicycle pump.

2. Fill the bottle three-quarters full with water. Put the smaller end of the cork into the bottle.

   CAUTION: Make sure that the cork is snug but not too tight. The cork must be loose enough to pop out when pressure is applied.

3. Lay the bottle on its side on the ground. Make sure that the bottom of the bottle is pointed away from people and toward an open outdoor area.

   CAUTION: Be sure to perform this activity outdoors and to point the rocket away from people, including yourself. All moving objects can cause injury if improperly used.

4. Use the bicycle pump to fill the bottle with air. You will see air bubbles coming out of the needle and into the water if your device is working correctly. Continue to fill the bottle until the air pressure in the bottle forces the cork to pop out. What happens?

More Fun Stuff to Do

Investigate how many pumps of air it takes to get the best launch. Do you always get a better launch with more pumps? Investigate how much water you need to get the best launch. Does more water mean a better flight? Make fins for your rocket out of cardboard. Do they help it fly?

Explanation

The Water Rocket flies because of Newton's Three Laws of Motion:

As with all rockets, it's Newton's third law—for every action, there is an equal and opposite reaction—that comes into play here. Air pressure forces the water out in one direction, and the rocket flies in the opposite direction. Increasing the air pressure does make the rocket fly better up to a point, but usually there is a limit to its effect as air begins to leak out of the cork.

Likewise, there is a limit to the amount of water used to launch the rocket. When you increase the amount of water, you also increase the weight that the rocket must carry during flight, so more water doesn't always mean a higher flight. A similar problem was faced when NASA engineers designed the rockets that put people on the moon. To get the extra thrust necessary for the trip, they couldn't just increase the amount of fuel, because that would have made the rocket too heavy to get off the ground. The engineers had to slightly increase the amount of fuel while slightly decreasing the overall weight of the rocket to obtain the best levels for flight. Fins added to a rocket help to keep it moving in a straight flight.

Water Wonder
WATERWHEELS

Humans have used the power of water for over 2,000 years. The earliest waterwheels were developed by the Greeks in the first century B.C. Their waterwheels used running water to turn paddles. The turning paddles turned grindstones, which ground grain into flour.

Waterwheels, like windmills, can be used to produce electricity. Try the following project to see how!

Project
WATERWHEEL

Much of the world's energy comes from **hydroelectricity** (electricity generated by the energy of falling water). But even before we learned how to generate electricity from water, we used waterwheels to do work for us. You can build your own waterwheel in this activity.

Materials

8 small plastic spoons or
   Popsicle sticks
Styrofoam ball
wire cutters or pliers (to be used
   only by an adult)
wire coat hanger
file (to be used only by an adult)

glue
two 1-inch (2.5-cm) pieces of
   plastic drinking straw
1-foot (30-cm) piece of string
bolt
sink
adult helper

Procedure

1. Push the spoons into the Styrofoam ball as shown. The spoons should all be facing in the same direction in a line around the middle of the ball. The spoons are the blades of the waterwheel.

2. Ask an adult to use the wire cutters to cut and straighten an 18-inch (45-cm) piece of wire from a coat hanger and file down any rough edges. This is the axle.

3. Insert the axle all the way through the center of the ball and out the other end so that there is an equal amount of wire on either side of the ball. Glue the wire in place. You have made a waterwheel.

4. Slide a piece of the straw onto each end of the axle. Hold the waterwheel by the straws so that you can see the inside of the bowls of the spoons. Blow on the blades. The blades should catch the wind and turn the waterwheel.

5. Tie one end of the string to the bolt. Tie the other end of the string to either side of the axle, attaching the string between the ball and the straw.

6. Grasp the straws of the axle and place the waterwheel in the sink so that the string and bolt hang down and the tips of the blades are directly under the tap.

7. Have an adult turn on the tap. What happens?

Explanation

Like the Windmill project in Chapter 2, in this project a turning machine uses kinetic energy from nature to do work. Water from the tap hits the blades of your Waterwheel, causing the blades to rotate about the axle. The energy of falling water is converted to the energy of the turning axle, which winds the string and raises the bolt.

If the axle is attached to an electric generator instead of to a string and bolt, the kinetic energy of the turning axle can be converted to electric energy. In hydroelectric power stations, falling water rotates a giant turning machine called a turbine, which powers an electric generator, producing large amounts of electricity.

Under Pressure
WATER PRESSURE INVENTIONS

Water, like air, is a fluid. Pascal's principle states that when a force is applied to one point of a fluid in a closed container, the force is transmitted equally to all parts of the fluid. Try the following project to investigate water pressure.

Project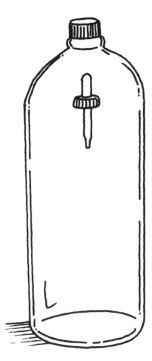
CARTESIAN DIVER

The Cartesian diver was first explained by René Descartes, a sixteenth-century French mathematician. Build a diver yourself to learn about water and water pressure.

Materials

eyedropper	½-gallon (2-liter) plastic soda
plastic drinking glass	bottle with screw-on lid
tap water	(empty and clean)

Procedure

1. Put the eyedropper in a glass of water to make sure that it floats. Squeeze the bulb end and draw in a small amount of water. If the eyedropper still floats, draw in more water. If it sinks, squeeze out some of the water. Keep drawing in or squeezing out water until the eyedropper just barely floats upright in the water.

2. Fill the bottle to the very top with water, making sure there are no air bubbles trapped inside the bottle.

3. Transfer the eyedropper to the bottle. Screw the lid tightly onto the bottle.

4. Gently squeeze the bottle. What happens? Relax your grip on the bottle. What happens?

Explanation

When you squeeze the bottle, the water pressure inside it increases, including the water pressure inside the eyedropper. You can actually see the level of water inside the eyedropper rise. As the water level inside the eyedropper rises, it squeezes the air in it into a smaller space. This pressure makes the eyedropper heavier than the water around it, and it sinks like a diver going to the bottom of the ocean.

When you relax your grip on the bottle, the pressure inside the bottle decreases and the air inside the eyedropper returns to its earlier level. The eyedropper becomes lighter than the surrounding water and starts to rise like a diver returning to the surface.

Sink or Swim
DENSITY INVENTIONS

Density is a physical property of objects. We use density to compare two substances that have equal **volume**, meaning they occupy the same amount of space, but have unequal masses, meaning they contain different amounts of matter. **Matter** is anything that has mass and occupies space. An object with more mass per volume is more dense than an object with less mass per volume. When put together, less dense substances will float on top of more dense substances.

Try the following activity and learn more about density.

Project
BOAT

It is easy to imagine how a wooden boat floats. Wood itself floats, so it makes sense to make a boat out of wood. But what about a boat made of steel? How does it float? Try the following activity to find out.

Materials

6-inch (15-cm) -square piece of aluminum foil
bathtub, sink, or any body of still water
pennies or marbles

Procedure

1. Fold up each edge of the foil about ½ inch (1.3 cm) to make a flat-bottomed boat. Fold back the extra foil to wrap around each corner so that no water gets in.

2. Place your boat in the bathtub. Does it float?

3. Add pennies to your boat one at a time until it sinks. Spread them out to evenly distribute the weight. How many can your boat hold?

More Fun Stuff to Do

Make another boat out of foil of the same size. This time fold up either more or less foil. See how many pennies or marbles this boat can hold. Experiment until you can design a boat out of the same size foil that holds the most pennies or marbles possible. What shape does the boat have?

Explanation

Objects float or sink depending on their density. Less dense objects will float on more dense substances. Water is very dense. Even a steel boat can float because its mass is less than the mass of an equal volume of water it displaces, or pushes out of place. As long as a boat has a mass that is less than an equal volume of water it displaces, it is less dense than water and will float on the surface.

A boat will be able to carry a cargo approximately equal in mass to the amount of water that the body of the boat displaces. What that means is that a boat the size of a cup will be able to carry a cargo that weighs almost the same as one cup of water. The actual amount of cargo carried will be slightly less because you have to include the weight of the boat in your calculations. In the More Fun Stuff to Do section, you probably discovered that your Boat could carry the most pennies if it was shaped like a cube. However, a cube does not move through the water very well.

What Time Is It?
WATER CLOCKS

Long before we had digital watches and electric clocks, people still needed to tell time. They used hourglasses, candle clocks, and a device called the water clock.

Make the following project to see how water can help you to tell time.

Project
WATER CLOCK

The water clock is an ancient device used for over 2,000 years to tell time. Galileo used this timing device when he studied the speed that an object falls to earth due to gravity. Try the following activity to make your own water clock.

Materials

small nail	tap water
2 see-through plastic containers (empty, clean cottage cheese containers or plastic milk cartons work well)	several books
	stopwatch
	marking pen
	helper
transparent tape	

Procedure

1. Use the nail to make a small hole in the bottom of one of the plastic containers. The hole should be between the center and the outer edge of the container. Place a piece of tape over the hole.

2. Place the books on the table, and place the second container next to the books. Fill the first container with water, and place it on the books so that the hole in the first container is over the second container.

3. Have your helper start the stopwatch as soon as you remove the tape. Water will begin to drip from the top container to the bottom container.

4. After 1 minute, use the marking pen to mark the level of the water in the container. Make sure to mark the bottom of the water curve. Continue to mark the water level every minute until all the water has dripped into the bottom container.

5. Tape the hole again, and refill the top container with the water from the bottom container. Place the bottom container under the top container. Remove the tape. You now have a water clock that tells time in minutes. You can estimate the time between the marks.

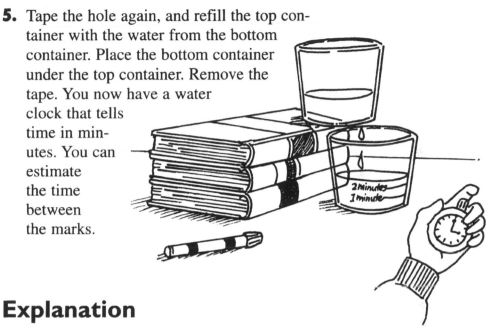

Explanation

The water clock works because of the fact that liquids flow at a constant rate out of a small hole. All timing devices, from the water clock to the digital watch, operate because of the fundamental principle that a regular pattern or cycle operates at a constant rate. In a water clock, the drops of water occur at a known rate that allows you to tell time. Likewise, the constant swing of a pendulum is used to tell time in a grandfather clock, and the regular vibrations of a quartz molecule are the basis of a digital watch. Even the rotation of the earth around the sun is used to tell time and this is how we determine the seasons and years.

Don't Be Shocked

If You're Attracted to These Activities

Using Electricity and Magnetism to Make Amazing Devices

Humans have been fascinated with electricity for thousands of years. The ancient Greeks noticed that if you rubbed amber—fossilized tree sap—with wool cloth, it would attract small bits of straw. Their experimentation led to the discovery of static electricity. Other famous scientists were also interested in electricity. Benjamin Franklin flew a kite in a thunderstorm to demonstrate the electrical nature of lightning, and Thomas Edison created the first lightbulb.

Almost everywhere you go you'll find electricity at work. Electricity is a form of energy that has many uses because it is easily changed into other forms of energy.

Electricity is a form of energy caused by the movement of one part of an atom, called the **electron.** All matter is made up of **atoms.** Atoms are made up of even smaller particles called **protons** and **neutrons,** which exist in the **nucleus,** or center, of the atom. The electrons orbit, or make a circular path around, the nucleus. In some materials, electrons can move from one atom to the next. This flow of electrons produces electricity. The movement of electrons around the nucleus also causes another phenomenon, called **magnetism**.

Try the following projects and activities to learn more about electricity and magnetism.

Short Circuit
GADGETS USING SIMPLE CIRCUITS

When you switch on a flashlight, you have just completed a simple electric circuit. An **electric circuit** is the path electrons take as they flow from the batteries, through the switch and bulb, and back to the batteries.

Try building your own simple circuits in the next two activities.

Project 1
COORDINATION TESTER

Try building an electric circuit that will test your coordination.

Materials

one 18-inch (45-cm) and one 6-inch (15-cm) piece of uninsulated wire (fuse wire, available at many hardware stores, works very well)

screwdriver

shoe box

wire strippers or pliers (to be used only by an adult)

two 8-inch (20-cm) and one 22-inch (55-cm) piece of insulated 22-gauge copper wire

electrical or transparent tape

4.5-volt lightbulb with bulb holder

6-volt dry-cell battery

adult helper

Procedure

1. Bend the 18-inch (45-cm) wire into a wavy line as shown. Make a 1-inch (2.5-cm) loop at one end of the 6-inch (15-cm) wire. Thread one end of the wavy wire through the loop.

2. With the screwdriver, make two holes in the lid of the shoe box about 8 inches (20 cm) apart, and push the ends of the wavy wire through the holes.

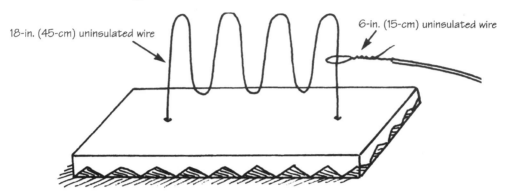

18-in. (45-cm) uninsulated wire

6-in. (15-cm) uninsulated wire

3. Have your adult helper use the wire strippers to strip 1 inch (2.5 cm) of insulation from the ends of the three insulated wires. Turn the box lid over, and wrap the end of one 8-inch (20-cm) wire around one end of the wavy wire. Tape the joined wires to the box lid. Tape the other end of the wavy wire to the box lid as well.

4. Place the lightbulb in the bulb holder. Take the free end of the 8-inch (20-cm) wire that is connected to the wavy wire and attach it to one connector of the bulb holder by wrapping it around the screw and tightening the screw with the screwdriver. Attach the remaining 8-inch (20-cm) wire to the other connector of the bulb holder in the same manner.

5. With the screwdriver, make a hole near the middle of the box lid big enough to fit the lightbulb through. Push the bulb up through the hole, and tape the bulb holder to the inside of the lid.

6. Take the free end of the 8-inch (20-cm) wire that is connected to the bulb and attach it to one of the battery terminals by wrapping the end of the wire around the terminal. Attach one end of the 22-inch (55-cm) wire to the other battery terminal in the same way.

6 VOLT BATTERY

7. Make a small hole in one corner of the box lid with the screw-driver, and push the free end of the 22-inch (55-cm) wire through it.

8. Put the battery in the box, and place the lid in place on top. The free end of the 22-inch (55-cm) wire should come through the hole in the box lid. Wrap the free end of the 22-inch (55-cm) wire to the end of the 6-inch (15-cm) wire loop. Your Coordination Tester is now ready.

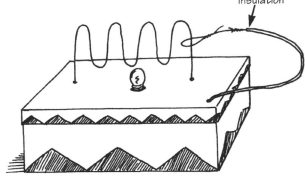

insulation

9. Holding on to the 22-inch (55-cm) wire, try to move the wire loop from one end of the wavy wire to the other without touching the wavy wire and making the bulb light up.

Project 2 ☀

DOORBELL

Now that you know how to wire an electric circuit, try making your own doorbell.

Materials

wire strippers or pliers (to be used only by an adult)
three 12-inch (30-cm) pieces of insulated 22-gauge copper wire

spring-type clothespin
6-volt dry-cell battery
6-volt bell or buzzer (available at a hardware store)
adult helper

Procedure

1. Have your adult helper use the wire strippers to remove ½ inch (1.3 cm) of insulation from the ends of all three insulated wires. Remove an additional 1 inch (2.5 cm) from one end of two of the wires.

2. Using the wires with the additional insulation removed, wind the longer stripped ends around each end of the clothespin. The wires should touch when the clothespin is pinched.

3. Attach the free end of one clothespin wire to the battery by wrapping it around one of the battery terminals. Attach the free end of the other clothespin wire to the bell by wrapping it around one of the bell terminal screws. Use the third wire to complete the circuit, wrapping one end around the other battery terminal and the other end around the other bell terminal screw.

4. Pinch the ends of the clothespin, and the bell should sound.

Explanation

In order to make electrons move, two things are needed: The first is a source of energy for the electrons. In these projects, the source of electrons is the chemical reaction that takes place inside the battery. The second thing needed is an electric circuit, a complete circular path. In every circuit that you make where the bulb lights up or the bell or buzzer rings, you should be able to trace a path from one battery terminal through the wires to the bulb or bell, back through the other wires, and ending at the opposite battery terminal.

In Project 1, Coordination Tester, you do not have a complete electric circuit unless you touch the loop of wire to the wavy wire. When you touch the loop to the wavy wire, you complete the circuit and the bulb lights up. In Project 2, Doorbell, the circuit is not complete until the wires in the clothespin touch. When you pinch the clothespin, the wires touch, making a circular path between the battery and the bell. Electricity flows from the battery to the bell and back, and your Doorbell sounds.

Fruit Energy
NATURAL BATTERIES

An **electric current** is caused by the movement of electrons through a complete circuit. One source of electrons is a **battery**. Batteries change the energy of a chemical reaction into electric energy. This electric energy can be used to light a flashlight, run a toy, or operate a clock. You will learn more about chemical reactions in Chapter 5.

In the following project, you'll make your own battery out of fruit!

Project
LEMON LIGHT

Try the following experiment to see how you can light a lightbulb with a battery made from a lemon!

Materials

½-by-2-inch (1.3-by-5-cm) copper strip
½-by-2-inch (1.3-by-5-cm) zinc strip
(copper and zinc strips are available at a hardware store)
hammer (to be used only by an adult)
nail
wire strippers or pliers (to be used only by an adult)

wires with alligator clips or two 12-inch (30 cm) -long insulated 22-gauge copper wires (wires with alligator clips make electrical activities easier and are available at most electronics stores)
lemon
0.2-volt lightbulb and holder or an LED (light-emitting diode) (available at most electronics stores)
adult helper

Procedure

1. If you're using insulated wires, have an adult helper first make a hole in one end of each metal strip, using the hammer and nail, and then use the wire strippers to strip 1 inch (2.5 cm) of insulation from the ends of the wires.

2. Insert the copper and zinc strips into the lemon about 1 inch (2.5 cm) apart.

3. Connect the alligator clips or one end of each wire to each of the strips. (Connect the insulated wires by threading the bare ends through the holes in the strips and wrapping the wire back on itself.) Connect the other alligator clips or ends of the wires to the wires on the lightbulb. What happens?

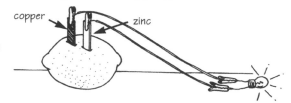

More Fun Stuff to Do

Place the strips farther apart or closer together, and observe the results. Experiment with using other types of metal strips or by substituting other fruits or vegetables. What happens?

Explanation

The electrical measurement **volt** is named after Alessandro Volta, an eighteenth-century Italian scientist. Volta discovered that certain chemical reactions could produce an electric current, which is a continuous flow of electrons. In order for the electrons to flow, a source of energy is needed. In the battery you created, the source of energy is the pair of metals. One metal has a tendency to lose electrons, while the other has a tendency to gain electrons. When these two metals are put into a chemical solution, such as the acid found in a lemon, electrons will move from one metal to the other.

When you use the wires to complete the circuit between the two metals, you are able to use the energy involved in the flow of electrons. This movement of electrons through the wires can light up a bulb or LED. The battery you created in this experiment is called a voltaic battery, also named for Alessandro Volta.

I'm Stuck on You
MAGNETISM

Everyone has observed a magnet attracting paper clips or other metal objects. Magnetism is an invisible source of attraction or repulsion between some substances. **Attraction** is the force that draws particles of matter together, while **repulsion** is the force that drives them apart. Magnetism, like electricity, is caused by the movement of electrons. Electrons moving in a wire create electricity, while electrons moving in orbit around the nucleus of an atom create magnetism.

Both electricity and magnetism are important in our daily lives. In the following project, you'll learn more about the magic of magnetism.

Project
ELECTROMAGNET

Try the following activity to learn more about electricity and magnetism.

Materials

1 yard (1 m) uninsulated
    22-gauge copper wire
16d nail

6-volt dry-cell battery
metal paper clip

Procedure

1. Coil the wire around the nail, leaving at least 6 inches (15 cm) of wire free at each end of the nail.

2. Attach one free end of the wire to the battery by wrapping the end of the wire around the terminal as shown.

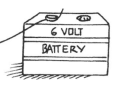

3. Bring the wrapped nail near the metal paper clip. What happens?

4. Attach the other free end of the wire to the battery by wrapping the end of the wire around the other terminal as shown.

5. Bring the nail with the coils of wire near the metal paper clip. What happens this time?

More Fun Stuff to Do

See how many paper clips you can pick up with your Electromagnet. What can you do to make your Electromagnet stronger? Try using a longer piece of wire and wrapping it around the nail more times. Substitute a bigger nail, several nails, or a large bolt.

Explanation

Electricity and magnetism are related. They share similar properties and are linked together as one of the four fundamental forces found in nature. Magnetism, like electricity, is caused by the movement of electrons. An electron is the part of an atom that orbits, or makes a circular path around, the nucleus, or center, of the atom. Electrons carry a negative charge and are capable of moving from one atom to another.

Although all matter is made of atoms with electrons in orbit around a nucleus, in magnetic objects all the atoms are lined up so that they point in the same direction. If they were large enough to see, they might look like thousands of spinning tops on a table. Each electron, spinning in orbit around the nucleus of the atom, creates a small **magnetic field**—the area around a magnet in which a magnetic force is felt. Together, these atoms lined up in the same direction and their spinning electrons become a magnetic material.

In nonmagnetic objects, the atoms arrange themselves randomly and their individual magnetism cancels out the magnetism of the other atoms.

Similarly, when electricity moves through a wire, it causes a magnetic field around the wire. When an electric current flows through a coil of wire, the coil acts like a magnet. This type of magnet is called an **electromagnet.** There are several ways to increase the power of the magnetic field around an electromagnet. You can increase the voltage of the battery, increase the number of coils of wire used, or change the type of metal around which the wire is coiled.

Where Am I?
COMPASSES

If you are ever lost, a **compass** can help you find your way. The magnetized needle of the compass always points north and south, because the earth acts as a natural magnet.

Project
COMPASS

Find your own way by making your own compass!

Materials

scissors
ruler
Styrofoam plate or other piece
   of flat Styrofoam (a packaged
     meat tray will work, but be sure
      to clean thoroughly before using)
2 needles
strong magnet

compass
marking pen
transparent tape
bowl
tap water

Procedure

1. Cut a 1-inch (2-cm) disk from the Styrofoam plate.

2. Magnetize one of the needles by rubbing it against a strong magnet 30 or 40 times. This works best if you always rub in the same direction. You can tell that the needle is magnetized when it attracts the other needle to it, just like a real magnet.

3. Insert the magnetized needle lengthwise through the disk.

4. Use the compass to determine north, south, east, and west. Write N, S, E, and W on pieces of tape, and stick the tape in the same locations on the bowl as they are on the compass.

5. Place the disk in a bowl of water. What happens? The needle should point north and south as it aligns itself with the earth's magnetic field.

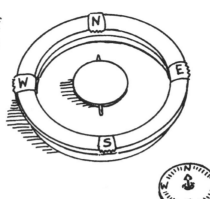

Explanation

All magnetism is caused by the movement of electrons. In a magnet, the spin of electrons in orbit around the nucleus of each atom creates the magnetic effect. Although all matter has electrons in orbit around a nucleus, in magnetic objects the atoms are all lined up so that they point in the same direction. By rubbing a nonmagnetic needle against a magnet, you cause the atoms in the needle to line up in the same direction, and the needle becomes magnetic.

The earth has a large magnetic field due to the movement of the molten magma—melted rock—in the earth's core. This magnetic field can be detected on the earth's surface with a magnet. The needle of a compass lines up automatically with the earth's magnetic field.

Great Chemistry

Using Chemistry to Make Cool Creations

We use chemistry in our lives every day. Even our bodies operate because of chemistry. Chemicals are in the foods we eat, the medicines we take, and the air we breathe.

The branch of science called **chemistry** is the investigation of matter, which is anything that has mass and occupies space. Chemistry includes studying how matter is used and how it changes in chemical reactions.

Don't Overreact!
CHEMICAL REACTIONS

A **chemical reaction** sounds like a mysterious thing, but it's simply the breaking apart of substances to make new substances.

Try the following chemical reactions, and see what new things you can make!

Project 1

GLUE

Glue is a sticky thing we use all the time. How is it made? Try the following activity and make some for yourself.

Materials

½ cup (125 ml) milk
1 tablespoon (15 ml) vinegar
saucepan
stove or hot plate (to be used only by an adult)
spoon
paper towel

strainer
plastic bowl
¼ teaspoon (1 ml) baking soda
tap water
2 sheets of paper
adult helper

NOTE: Procedure requires a stove or hot plate and adult supervision.

Procedure

1. Place the milk and the vinegar in the saucepan. Have an adult gently warm the mixture on the stove while you stir occasionally with the spoon. The milk will turn into two substances: curds (the solid part) and whey (the liquid part).

2. Place the paper towel in the strainer. Hold the strainer over the bowl, and have an adult pour the heated mixture through the strainer. The whey will flow through the strainer into the bowl, while the curds will remain in the strainer.

3. Pour the curds from the strainer back into the pan, and add the baking soda. Stir gently. Don't be surprised if the baking soda reacts with any leftover vinegar by bubbling.

4. Slowly add water to the curds, a teaspoon at a time, until the mixture thickens. You have made glue!

5. Test your glue by pasting two sheets of paper together.

Project 2
COIN CLEANER

If your pennies are looking dull, use some simple chemistry to shine them.

Materials

½ cup (125 ml) lemon juice   timer
small jar or juice glass   paper towel
several dull, dirty pennies

Procedure

1. Pour the lemon juice into the jar.

2. Place the pennies in the juice, and soak them for about 5 minutes.

3. Fish out the coins, and place them on the paper towel to dry. What happened to the pennies?

Project 3 ☼
ELECTROCHEMICAL PLATING MACHINE

If you have ever wondered how a chrome bumper is made, try the following activity to see how it can be done.

Materials

½ cup (125 ml) lemon juice   nail
small jar or juice glass   scouring pad
15 to 20 dull copper pennies   scouring powder
pinch of salt   tap water
timer   paper towel

Procedure

1. Pour the lemon juice into the jar.

2. Place the pennies in the juice.

3. Add a pinch of salt to the juice. Let the pennies stand in the solution for 2 or 3 minutes.

4. Meanwhile, use the scouring pad to clean the nail with scouring powder and water. When it is very clean, add the nail to the solution with the pennies. Leave the nail in the solution for at least 15 minutes.

5. Take the nail out of the solution, and place it on the paper towel to dry. What happened to the nail?

Explanation

These three projects are all examples of chemical reactions. In Project 1, Glue, you combine two substances, milk and vinegar, to make a new substance, glue. First, you use the vinegar, an acid, to sour the milk. The milk breaks down into two new substances, curds and whey. The curds are made of casein, a protein found in milk. When you add baking soda to the curds, you create another chemical reaction with the remaining vinegar. This reaction results in another new substance, casein glue, a sticky protein.

In Project 2, Coin Cleaner, a chemical reaction is used to clean pennies. Oxygen in the air combines with the copper in pennies to form a copper oxide coating that makes your pennies look dull and dirty. When you place the dull, dirty pennies in the lemon juice, you create a chemical reaction. The acid of the lemon juice acts chemically to remove the copper oxide. The result is pennies that look like new.

Two chemical reactions occur in Project 3, Electrochemical Plating Machine. First, the copper from the pennies reacts with the acid of the lemon juice to form a new substance, copper citrate. When you place the nail in the solution, a second reaction occurs. The copper citrate compound plates, or covers, the nail with a thin layer of copper that cannot be rubbed off. This process is called **electrochemical plating**.

Chemical Power
REACTIONS AND NEWTON'S LAWS

Whenever a chemical reaction takes place, new substances are made. Often these new substances have properties totally unlike the original substances. Sometimes the new substances, called products, have explosive properties!

Try the following project to see for yourself.

Project
KODAK CANNON

A little bit of chemistry and Newton's laws of motion can make a car move.

Materials

safety glasses	Alka-Seltzer tablet
newspaper	transparent tape
empty plastic film canister with lid	2-inch (5-cm) -long toy car or truck
tap water	

Procedure

1. Put on the safety glasses. Cover your table or work area with newspaper.

2. Fill the film canister half full with water.

3. Break the Alka-Seltzer tablet of into quarters. Place one quarter of the tablet in the canister. Do not put the top on the canister. What happens when the tablet touches the water?

4. Empty the canister, and refill it with fresh water.

5. Place a quarter tablet of Alka-Seltzer in the canister. Quickly and firmly put the lid on the canister. Set the "loaded" canister down and move at least 3 feet (1 m) away from it. What happens to the canister?

6. Empty the canister again. Tape the canister to the back of the toy car so that the open end of the canister is at the rear end of the car as shown.

Alka-Seltzer

7. Turn the canister upright, and fill it half full with water. Add a quarter tablet of Alka-Seltzer and secure the lid onto the canister. Place the wheels of the car on a table or floor, and move at least 3 feet (1 m) away. What happens to the car?

More Fun Stuff to Do

Experiment with greater or smaller amounts of Alka-Seltzer and water to see if you can get the car to go faster or farther.

Explanation

This is an example of a chemical reaction that produces explosive results. The Alka-Seltzer tablet contains a substance called bicarbonate. When you mix bicarbonate with water, a new substance, carbon dioxide gas, is formed. When you put the lid on the canister, the carbon dioxide gas is trapped. The pressure of the gas builds up until it is strong enough to pop the lid off the canister.

Newton's laws of motion come into play in the second part of the experiment when you tape the canister to the car. Newton's third law of motion states that for every action there is an equal and opposite reaction. The lid popping off the canister is the action. That action then causes an equal and opposite reaction in the canister. It moves off in the opposite direction, taking the car with it.

So Cool!
ENDOTHERMIC REACTIONS

As you know, chemical reactions involve breaking down substances to make new substances. Energy is used to break down old substances, and it is released when new substances are made. Often the energy involved in chemical reactions takes the form of heat.

Chemical reactions that give off heat are called **exothermic** reactions, while those that absorb heat are called **endothermic** reactions. The lighting of a match is an example of an exothermic reaction. The burning process releases energy that we feel as heat. But endothermic chemical reactions get colder, as you'll discover in the next experiment.

Project
COLD PACK

Try this activity to see an endothermic reaction in action.

Materials

safety glasses
measuring cup
tap water
several Ziploc plastic
  bags

2 tablespoons (30 ml) sodium thiosulfate
  (also called photographer's hypo,
  available from photography supply
  stores) (to be used only by an adult)
adult helper

CAUTION: Follow all instructions written on the bottle. Do not touch the sodium thiosulfate.

Procedure

1. Put on the safety glasses. Pour ½ cup (125 ml) of water into the bag to determine if there are any leaks. If the bag leaks, try several bags until you find one with no leaks. Empty the water from the bag.

2. Have an adult put the sodium thiosulfate in the nonleaking bag.

3. Feel the bottom of the bag to observe its temperature.

4. Slowly add another ½ cup (125 ml) of water to the bag. Close the top of the bag carefully so that none of the solution spills out. Mix the solution thoroughly by gently shaking the bag.

5. Feel the bag again. What happened to the temperature during the reaction?

Explanation

In this activity you have created your own cold pack. You may have used a cold pack or seen one used when a player is injured during an athletic event. Cold packs are an example of an endothermic reaction, a chemical reaction that takes heat, a form of energy, from its surroundings. The sodium thiosulfate crystals require energy to dissolve. They take that energy from the water by taking the heat out of the water. As energy is transferred from the water to the crystals to help them dissolve, the water loses heat and its temperature decreases.

Testing One, Two, Three
CHEMICAL INDICATORS

Chemistry can be used to test chemicals in order to identify them or learn more about them. **Chemicals** are substances that can change when mixed with other substances. Every chemical reacts differently depending on its properties. Chemicals have different melting points, are different colors, and may or may not combine with certain other chemicals.

Substances called **indicators** can be used to tell whether a chemical is an **acid** or **base**. Acids and bases are opposites, and when mixed together they can neutralize each other, or cancel each other out. Indicators, such as **litmus,** turn different colors when mixed with an acid or base. Acids turn litmus red, while bases turn litmus blue.

Try the following activity to learn more about chemical indicators.

Project
CABBAGE JUICE INDICATOR

The juice from red cabbage is a typical chemical indicator.

Materials

red cabbage
2-quart (2-liter) saucepan
2 quarts (2 liters) tap water
stove or hot plate
timer
colander
plastic bowl
5 small jars

marking pen
measuring cup
1 teaspoon (5 ml) lemon juice
1 teaspoon (5 ml) vinegar
1 teaspoon (5 ml) distilled water
1 teaspoon (5 ml) baking soda
1 tsp. (5 ml) ammonia
adult helper

NOTE: Procedure requires a stove or hot plate and adult supervision.

Procedure

1. Tear two red cabbage leaves into small pieces, and place them in the saucepan with the 2 quarts (2 liters) of water.

2. Ask an adult to set the pan on the stove and boil the cabbage leaves for 5 minutes.

3. Hold the colander over the bowl, and have an adult strain the leaves through the colander. Throw the leaves away. Allow the colored liquid to cool in the bowl.

4. Number the jars 1 through 5 with the marking pen.

5. Pour ½ cup (125 ml) of the cooled cabbage juice into each of the 5 small jars.

6. Add the lemon juice to jar 1, the vinegar to jar 2, the distilled water to jar 3, the baking soda to jar 4, and the ammonia to jar 5.

CAUTION: Be careful not to spill the ammonia on your hands.

7. Observe the color that each chemical turns the cabbage juice, and record the color on a chart similar to the one shown.

82

Jar	Chemical	Acid/Base	Color
1	lemon juice	acid	
2	vinegar	slightly acid	
3	distilled water	neutral	
4	baking soda	slightly base	
5	ammonia	base	

More Fun Stuff to Do

Make cabbage juice litmus paper by soaking a coffee filter in 1 cup (250 ml) of the cabbage juice. Allow the paper to dry on a piece of newspaper or paper towel, and then cut it into strips. On each of 5 strips of paper, put a drop of each chemical listed in the chart, and note the color. The results with litmus paper should be the same as those in the project. The remaining papers can be used to test other chemicals.

Use the remaining cabbage juice to test foods in your kitchen, such as milk, pickle juice, soy sauce, and baking powder. Set up new jars of cabbage juice, and add small amounts of food. Observe the color the juice becomes. Compare the color the juice becomes to the colors recorded on your chart. Use the colors to determine whether the food is acid, slightly acid, neutral, slightly base, or base.

Test the rain in your area. Is it acidic? Do you have a problem with acid rain or snow? Test the rain at different times of the year. Does it change?

Explanation

When a chemical indicator is mixed with an acid or a base, a chemical reaction occurs. The exact reason an indicator changes color when mixed with an acid or base has been studied for many years. It appears that the acid or base changes the structure of the atoms of the indicator by changing the way the electrons of the acid or base fit around the nucleus of its atoms. This causes the change in color of the indicator.

Cabbage juice is a chemical indicator that changes color depending on the type of solution added. The following are the expected results for this activity:

Jar	Chemical	Acid/Base	Color
1	lemon juice	acid	red
2	vinegar	slightly acid	pink
3	distilled water	neutral	dark purple
4	baking soda	slightly base	light green
5	ammonia	base	green

Strings and Things

Using Acoustics to Build Dynamite Devices

Sit quietly and listen to the sounds that are all around you. Sound travels through the air just as ripples travel across a pond when a stone is thrown into the middle of it. The water near the stone vibrates—moves up and down—while the ripples travel outward in small waves.

Sounds are vibrations that travel in **sound waves**. Humans can hear certain vibrations. Other vibrations, such as dog whistles, can be heard by animals but are too high or too low for humans to hear. The property of sound that makes it high or low is called **pitch**. A high-pitched sound has more sound waves traveling over a given time, so the sound waves have a higher **frequency**.

The branch of science that investigates sound is called **acoustics**. Try the following activities to learn more about sound.

Now Hear This!
MACHINES THAT CARRY SOUND

The sounds of the world are carried in the form of sound energy. **Sound** is the form of energy that lets us hear. Sound energy travels in waves and can travel through matter, meaning through gases, such as air, or through liquids and solids.

The loudness of a sound depends on the amount of energy carried by the sound wave. This is called **amplitude**. We can use machines, like amplifiers, to increase or decrease the amplitude of a sound. Mechanical devices like the ones you'll make in the following projects can help you hear sounds better.

Project 1
YOGURT CUP PHONES

A simple way to investigate sound is to use homemade telephones. Try the following project, and build a set for yourself.

Materials

small nail
candle or other flame (to be used only by an adult)
pliers (to be used only by an adult)

2 small plastic yogurt containers (empty and clean)
5-yard (5-m) string
adult helper
helper

Procedure

1. Ask an adult to hold the nail over the candle flame with pliers and heat the nail, then use the heated nail to melt a small hole in the bottom of each of the plastic containers.

2. Thread one end of the string through one of the holes in one container. Tie a large knot so that the string can't be pulled back through the hole. Do the same with the other end of the string and the other container.

3. Have a helper take one of the containers into another room, trailing the string behind him or her, while you hold the other container. The string should be straight and stretched taut.

4. Take turns talking into one container while the other person puts the other container to his or her ear. How well does your phone system work?

More Fun Stuff to Do ☼

Try other containers, such as plastic or paper cups and tin cans of various sizes. Which containers work the best? Try other types of string, such as thread, nylon fishing line, or dental floss. Which material works the best? Try to design the best phone system possible.

Try making the string longer or shorter. What is the longest that the string can be and still have the phone system work properly?

Combine two phone systems. Can you make a system that several people can use at one time?

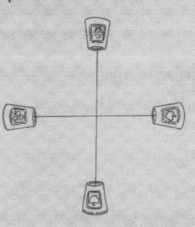

Project 2 ☀
TIN CAN HOWLER

The tin can howler is a popular toy found in Spain and other parts of Europe. The scientific principles used to construct it are also used in making musical instruments. Build several howlers for yourself and see what different sounds you can make.

Materials

hammer (to be used only by an adult)
nail
tin can (empty and clean)

2-foot (60-cm) piece of string
tap water
adult helper

Procedure

1. Ask an adult to make a small hole with the hammer and nail in the center of the bottom of the tin can.

2. Thread the string through the hole. Knot the string inside the can so that the string can't be pulled back through the hole.

3. Wet the string with water.

4. Grasp the string near the can, and pull your hand down the string, holding the string taut. You may need to rub the string with your thumb or thumbnail to get the best results. What happens?

More Fun Stuff to Do ☀

Try this activity using different-sized cans and different types of string. What effect does a different-sized can have on the sound you can create? Do other kinds of string work?

Project 3 ○

FUNNEL STETHOSCOPE

Machines can be used to make sounds traveling through air louder or softer. The **stethoscope** is a device used to make the sounds of your body loud enough to hear.

Materials

1-yard (1 m) rubber tubing   funnel
  (available at most   tape
  drugstores)

Procedure

1. Fit one end of the rubber tubing over the narrow end of the funnel. You may need to use tape if the funnel does not fit tightly in the tube.

2. Hold the free end of the tubing next to your ear, and place the wide end of the funnel over your heart.

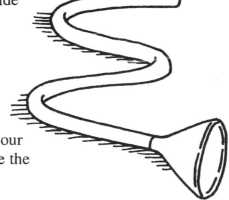

3. What do you hear? Don't worry if you don't hear anything right away. You may have to move the funnel to several locations on your chest to find the place where the heartbeat is the loudest.

More Fun Stuff to Do ○

Listen to other people's hearts by asking them to hold the funnel against their chest.

Explanation

Sound can travel through gases, like air, as well as through solid materials. In the preceding activities, you have investigated both. In Project 1, Yogurt Cup Phones, the sound is caused by your voice. In Project 2, Tin Can Howler, the sound is caused by the movement of the string. In both activities, the sound vibrations travel through a solid, the string. The yogurt cups and the tin can act as cavities that **amplify** (make louder) the sound. A cavity helps to amplify the sound, because sound waves inside the cavity hit the walls of the container, bounce back, and reinforce each other. This process of enriching sound with supplementary vibrations is called **resonance**.

In Project 3, Funnel Stethoscope, the sound is caused by the beating of your heart, and it travels through the air. The funnel directs the sound vibrations into the tube so they can more easily travel through the air and into your ear.

Music to My Ears
MUSICAL INSTRUMENTS

Musical instruments work by making air vibrate. Musicians play tunes and make rhythms by controlling the sounds the instruments make. The sound an instrument makes depends on the way the instrument vibrates the air and how the vibration interacts with the instrument itself.

Make the instruments in this section to learn more about sounds. When you're done, you'll be able to start your own musical band!

Project 1
WHISTLE

Try the following activity and investigate sound.

Materials

scissors
2 drinking straws, one slightly thinner than the other
   (paper ones work best)

Procedure

1. Cut a notch in one end of the thinner straw to make a point as shown.

2. Flatten the cut end of the straw with your thumbnail, then separate the point to create a small slit.

3. Put the pointed end between your lips and blow as hard as you can. What happens?

4. Place the wider straw around the first one. Move the outer straw up or down to change the length of your instrument. Blow on the inner straw. What happens to the sound?

More Fun Stuff to Do ☼

Using only the cut straw, have a friend cut small pieces off the straw as you blow. How does this affect the sound?

Project 2 ☼
PAPER TUBE KAZOO

There are other ways to make music. Can you make a kazoo? Try the following project to find out.

Materials

3-inch (7.5-cm) circular piece of tissue paper
cardboard tube (such as the tube inside a toilet paper roll)
rubber band
pencil

Procedure

1. Place the circle of tissue paper over one end of the tube, and secure it with a rubber band.

2. Use the pencil to punch a hole in the side of the tube near the end that is covered with paper.

3. Hum or sing into the open end of the tube. What happens?

Project 3
GUITAR

Vibrating strings and a sound box are all you need to build a guitar. Try building a simple guitar to learn how it works.

Materials

10 rubber bands
tin loaf pan
scissors
ruler
4 wire brads

large plastic yogurt or cottage
    cheese container (empty and clean)
2-by-12-inch (5-by-30-cm)
    piece of cardboard

Procedure

Part 1

1. Place 8 of the rubber bands around the loaf pan, spacing them evenly.

2. Pluck each rubber band individually. What sounds do they make?

3. Tighten or loosen the fit of the rubber bands by changing how they stretch across the opening of the pan. Observe the effect on the sound produced.

4. Try adjusting the rubber bands so that you can play the musical scale of do, re, mi, fa, sol, la, ti, and back to do.

Part 2

1. Cut a slot 2 inches (5 cm) wide on one side of the plastic container. Cut an identical slot on the opposite side of the container.

2. Insert the piece of cardboard through both slots.

3. Insert 2 wire brads through each end of the cardboard. Stretch the remaining 2 rubber bands over the container, and loop the ends of the rubber bands around the wire brads.

4. Pluck your guitar. How does it sound?

More Fun Stuff to Do ☼

To play both guitars together, stretch and loosen the rubber bands so that both instruments make similar sounds when plucked. Use either guitar to try playing a song!

Explanation

All of the instruments you made create sound by vibrating the air. When you blow inside the Whistle in Project 1, the vibration of the cut end of the straw creates the sound by causing the column of air in the straw to vibrate. The length of this column of air determines the pitch, which is the property of sound that makes it high or low. By sliding the second straw up or down over the cut straw, you change the length of the column of air, and this changes the pitch of the notes you play.

In Project 2, Paper Tube Kazoo, the sound waves that you produce by humming or singing vibrate the tissue paper at the other end of the tube. This vibration produces the unusual kazoo sound.

The strings of the Guitar in Project 3 vibrate and produce sound when you pluck them. Like the Yogurt Cup Phones and the Tin Can Howler of the previous section, the Guitar uses a cavity to amplify the sound. The size and shape of the cavity has a great effect on the sound that is produced. The tautness and length of the strings (rubber bands) also influence the sound produced. Shorter and tauter strings vibrate at higher frequencies and produce higher-pitched notes. Longer and looser strings vibrate at lower frequencies and produce lower-pitched notes.

Lighten Up!

Using Optics to Create Fantastic Fun

7

Light is the form of energy that lets us see. Light comes from many sources, from the sunlight we see in the morning to the electric lights we turn on at night. Light is **reflected**—bounced back—off some objects. The color an object appears is the part of light that is reflected by that object. All other colors are absorbed.

Optics is the area of science that studies light. Learn more about light in the following activities.

Mirror, Mirror
REFLECTION INVENTIONS

Every time you look in the mirror, you are experimenting with light. Have you ever wondered how a mirror works? Why is the image you see in a mirror reversed? Why do some mirrors make you look funny?

Mirrors reflect light. When a beam of light hits a mirrored surface, it is reflected off the mirror at the same angle. Try the following activities and see how much fun you can have with light, mirrors, and reflections.

Project 1
KALEIDOSCOPE

A **kaleidoscope** uses mirrors to create multiple reflections of colored objects inside a tube in an endless variety of patterns. It is great fun and is full of science. Try building your own to see how it works.

Materials

1-quart (1-liter) cardboard milk carton (empty and clean)
and
mirrored Con-Tact paper (available at many hardware stores)
or
three 2-by-8-inch (5-by-20-cm) mirrors (available cut to size at many glass stores)

transparent tape
scissors
two 4-inch (10-cm) -square pieces of plastic wrap
2 rubber bands
pieces of colored paper
beads

Procedure

1. If you are using the milk carton and mirrored Con-Tact paper:

   a. Cut off the top, bottom, and one side of the milk carton so that you have three connected panels.

b. Cut a piece of Con-Tact paper the same size as the combined three panels of the milk carton. Stick the Con-Tact paper on the inside of the carton.

c. Fold the three panels into a triangular tube with the shiny part inside. Secure the panels to each other with tape.

2. If you are using three mirrors, tape the long sides of the mirrors together to make a triangular tube with the shiny part inside.

3. Set the triangular tube upright on a table, and cover one end with one of the pieces of plastic wrap. Secure the plastic with a rubber band. Place the pieces of paper and beads on the plastic wrap.

4. Cover the paper and beads with the other piece of plastic wrap, and secure it with the other rubber band.

5. Look through the open end of the kaleidoscope to see what beauty it creates. Every time you move or turn it, the shapes should change.

Project 2 ☼
PERISCOPE

You have probably seen a **periscope** in a movie about submarines. The commander of the submarine can see what is happening on the surface of the water without ever coming up. It is all done with mirrors. Build the next project to see around corners and above crowds.

Materials

scissors
two 1-quart (1-liter) cardboard
    milk cartons (empty
    and clean)
transparent tape
ruler

protractor
pencil
two small mirrors at least
    3 inches (7.5 cm) square
    (available cut to size at many
    glass stores)

Procedure

1. Cut off the top and bottom of each milk carton.

2. Tape the ends of the two cartons together so that they form a long tube.

3. Place the tube upright on a table. Cut a 2-inch (5-m) -square opening in one side at one end of the tube. Cut another 2-inch (5-cm) -square opening in the opposite side at the other end of the tube as shown.

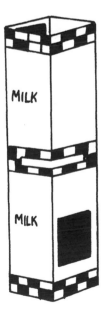

4. With the protractor, measure 45-degree angles on the sides adjacent to each square. To do this, place the center of the protractor on one corner of the tube, next to the side with the square opening. Use the pencil to make a mark on the tube at 45 degrees. Use the ruler to draw a line from the corner of the tube to the mark. Repeat for the corner next to the other square.

5. Cut two ⅛-by-3-inch (0.3-by-7.5-cm) slots along the 45-degree marks.

6. Slide the mirrors into the slots. The shiny sides must face each other. Tape the mirrors to the tube to hold them in place.

7. Hold your tube upright, and look into one of the square holes. You should be able to see over the heads of people or things that are taller than you. If you hold your periscope sideways, you'll be able to see around corners.

shiny sides of mirror facing

Project 3 ☀
FUN HOUSE MIRROR

Have you ever been to an amusement park and seen yourself in a curvy mirror at the fun house? Why not make one for yourself? Your reflection can be stretched or squeezed, depending on how you make the mirror.

Materials

8-by-12-inch (20-by-30-cm) piece
   of mirrored Con-Tact paper
   (available at many hardware stores)
8-by-12-inch (20-by-30-cm) piece
   of cardboard

Procedure

1. Stick the mirrored Con-Tact paper on the cardboard.

2. Observe your image. What can you see?

3. Bend the top and bottom edges of the cardboard toward you. What happens to your image?

4. Bend the top and bottom edges of the cardboard away from you. What happens to your image?

5. Bend the cardboard in an S shape, with the top edge toward you and the bottom edge away from you. What happens to your image?

Explanation

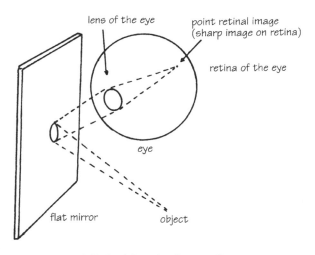

lens of the eye

point retinal image
(sharp image on retina)

retina of the eye

eye

flat mirror

object

All of the projects in this
section work because of
mirrors. Mirrors reflect
light. When you look in a
regular, flat mirror, light
hitting the mirror bounces
off it at an angle equal to
the angle at which it went
in. (That's one simple law
of reflected light: It is
reflected at the same angle
at which it went in.) When the reflected light hits the lens of your
eye, the lens focuses the image at one point on your eye's retina,
creating a **point retinal image** as shown. The image is clear.

Both the Kaleidoscope and the Periscope in Projects 1 and 2 use
several flat mirrors. In the Kaleidoscope, images of the colored
paper and beads are reflected several times as they travel along the
mirrored tube to your eye. We see these multiple images as beauti-
ful patterns. With the Periscope, the image you see bounces off one
mirror, is reflected on the other, and then bounces off the second
mirror and onto the lens of your eye.

The Fun House Mirror in Project 3 is a curved mirror. Light tries to
bounce off a curved mirror at an angle equal to the angle at which it
went in, but instead it gets bounced off in unusual angles. The lens
of your eye tries to focus the light bouncing off the curved mirror,
but it can't quite do it. Rather than cause all the light, and therefore
the image, to focus at one point on the lens, the curved mirror causes the image to spread out and be blurred. The place where the lens

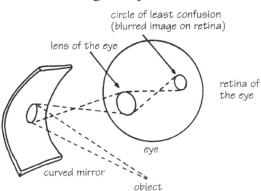

circle of least confusion
(blurred image on retina)

lens of the eye

retina of
the eye

eye

curved mirror

object

focuses the blurred image on
the retina is called the
circle of least confusion.
The brain tries to interpret that
image as best it can, and we
see the distorted, confused
image of the Fun House
Mirror.

Say Cheese!
CAMERAS

With the snap of a picture, you can save a moment in time forever. Have you ever wondered how cameras work?

All cameras produce images by focusing light onto film. Try making your own camera to see how it works.

Project
SHOE BOX CAMERA

Build your own camera out of a shoe box.

Materials

scissors
ruler
shoe box
transparent tape

aluminum foil
waxed paper
pin

Procedure

1. Cut a 1-inch (2.5-cm) -square hole in one end of the shoe box. Tape a piece of aluminum foil over the hole. Make sure all edges of the foil are taped to the box.

2. Cut the opposite end off the shoe box.

3. Put the lid on the shoe box, and tape it in place.

4. Tape a piece of waxed paper over the end of the shoe box that has been removed.

5. Use the pin to make a small hole in the center of the aluminum foil.

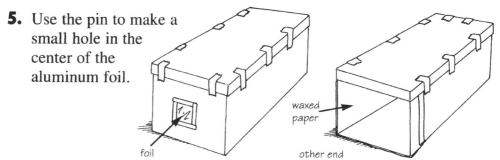

foil

waxed paper

other end

6. Point the pinhole end of the shoe box at a window or other light source. Look at the waxed paper end of the shoe box. An image of what is before you will pass through the pinhole and appear on the waxed paper. What do you see?

Explanation

Cameras, including your Shoe Box Camera, work by focusing the correct amount of light onto a screen to form an image. If there is film on the screen, the image can be permanently recorded. Cameras work because light travels in a straight line.

In your camera, light travels in straight lines that cross as they pass through the pinhole and onto the waxed paper screen. Light from the top of the object travels in a straight line through the pinhole and onto the bottom of the waxed paper, while light from the bottom of the object lands on the top of the paper. Therefore, the image you see on the paper is upside down.

Lights, Camera, Action!
MOVING PICTURES

Ever since my first visit to a movie theater, I've been fascinated with cartoons and movies. Did you know that cartoons and movies are actually still drawings and photographs recorded on film by cameras and projected rapidly onto a screen? It's **vision**, the way your eyes and brain work together, that make you believe the images on the screen are moving. Try the following projects to learn more.

Project 1 ☼
THAUMATROPE

One of the earliest ways to make moving pictures was a simple toy called the **thaumatrope**. This gadget makes images move so fast that you can see an object that is out-of-sight! Try making one for yourself.

Materials

crayons or markers
two 4-inch (10-cm) -square
   pieces of white paper
transparent tape

two 4-inch (10-cm) -square
   pieces of cardboard
pencil

Procedure

1. With crayons, draw a picture of a bird on one piece of paper and a picture of a bird-cage on the other piece of paper.

2. Tape the drawings to the pieces of cardboard.

3. Tape the back of one piece of cardboard to the pencil. Then tape the other piece of cardboard back-to-back against the first piece of cardboard as shown.

4. Roll the pencil between your hands so that the pictures spin. Observe the two drawings. What happens?

More Fun Stuff to Do

Think of other pairs of pictures that can come together to make one picture, like a picture of a boat and a picture of the ocean. See how many different thaumatropes you can make.

Project 2

FLIP BOOK

By making a flip book, you can actually make your own movie!

Materials

small pad of paper with a gummed edge
    (available at stationery stores)
pencil

Procedure

1. Before you start making your movie, you will first need to decide what it will be about. Start out with a simple idea: for example, a boy shooting a basketball, a seed growing into a flower, or an ant walking across the page.

2. Make at least 25 drawings to bring your movie to life. Start by making your first drawing on the last page on your pad, because it is easier to flip the pad from back to front.

3. Turn to the next-to-last page. You will probably be able to see the previous drawing through the page, which will help you with your next one. Make your next drawing slightly different from the first one.

4. Continue drawing pictures on each page until your movie is done, making each drawing slightly different from the one before.

5. To view the movie, hold the gummed edge of the pad in your right hand and flip through it quickly with your left hand, from the last page to the first.

Explanation

Both the Thaumatrope and the Flip Book are cases of the hand being quicker than the eye. Your eye sees the first drawing for a fraction of a second, and then the drawing disappears. The next drawing appears before your eyes have a chance to react. The first image is retained on the retina of your eye for a fraction of a second in a process called **persistence of vision**.

Images received on the retina actually remain there for $\frac{1}{16}$ second. As a result of persistence of vision, you do not see two separate images but one image that contains both drawings. In the Thaumatrope, the effect is that you see one object combined from both drawings. In the Flip Book, the effect is that you see objects that appear to move.

Glossary

acceleration Increasing speed.

acid A type of chemical that reacts with a base to form salt and water. It turns litmus red.

acoustics The study of sound.

air The gas that surrounds us.

air pressure The pressure exerted by air.

amplify To make a sound louder.

amplitude The loudness of a sound determined by the amount of energy carried by the sound wave.

atom The smallest part of matter.

attraction The electric or magnetic force that draws particles of matter together.

base A type of chemical that reacts with an acid to form salt and water. It turns litmus blue.

battery A device that can convert the energy of a chemical reaction into electricity.

Bernoulli's principle The natural law that states that when any fluid, such as air, flows, its pressure decreases as its speed increases.

center of mass The point in an object where its mass is equal in all directions.

chemical reaction A change in matter in which substances break apart to produce one or more new substances.

chemicals Substances that can change when mixed with other substances.

chemistry The science that investigates matter.

circle of least confusion The area where a blurred image hits the retina.

compass A device that allows you to find the direction north using a free-swinging magnetized needle.

compress To push together.

condense To change from a gas to a liquid.

density A physical property of matter that is determined by dividing the mass of an object by its volume.

elastic energy The potential energy stored in a material when its shape is changed by either stretching or compressing.

electric circuit A complete pathway for an electric current, from the source and back again.

electric current A continuous flow of electrons in a complete electric circuit.

electricity A form of energy that comes from the moving of electrons.

electrochemical plating The chemical reaction of metal molecules in solution with another metal. The metal molecules will plate (or coat) the other metal due to the transfer of electrons.

electromagnet A magnet produced by an electric current flowing through a coiled wire.

electron A small, negatively charged subatomic particle that moves in orbit around the nucleus of an atom.

endothermic A chemical reaction characterized by the absorption of heat energy from the surroundings.

energy The ability to do work.

evaporate To change from a liquid to a gas.

exothermic A chemical reaction characterized by the release of heat energy into the surroundings.

fluid A state of matter, either liquid or gas, in which the particles are free to move from one place to another.

force A push or pull on an object.

frequency The number of times an event, such as a sound wave, occurs in a given length of time.

friction A force that works in an opposite direction to an object that is moving along a surface.

fulcrum The fixed support point of a lever.

generator A machine that uses magnetism to convert kinetic energy into electricity.

gravity The force that pulls objects toward the earth.

gyroscopic effect The tendency of a rotating object to have a more stable flight that an object that doesn't spin.

hydroelectricity Electricity generated by the energy of falling water.

hypothesis An educated guess about the results of an experiment.

indicator A chemical substance that changes color when placed in an acid or base solution.

kaleidoscope A device that uses mirrors to create multiple reflections of colored objects inside a tube in an endless variety of patterns.

kinetic energy The energy of an object in motion.

lever   A simple machine made up of a rigid board or bar that is supported at a fixed point called a fulcrum.

light   The form of energy that lets us see.

litmus   An indicator that changes color when placed in an acid or base solution.

machine   A device that helps you do work more easily.

magnetic field   The area around a magnet in which a magnetic force is felt.

magnetism   The form of energy that causes some substances to attract or repel other substances.

mass   The amount of material an object contains.

matter   Anything that has mass and occupies space.

mechanics   The study of machines and how they work.

molecule   A particle made up of two or more joined atoms.

neutron   An uncharged subatomic particle found in the nucleus of an atom.

Newton's three laws of motion   Three laws that govern the motion of objects. They are: (1) An object at rest will stay at rest and an object in motion will stay in motion, unless they are acted upon by an outside force; (2) An object will move with an acceleration that is proportional to the force applied to it; and (3) For every action, there is an equal and opposite reaction.

nucleus   The center of the atom, which consists of varying numbers of protons and neutrons.

optics   The study of light.

Pascal's principle   The natural law that states that when a force is applied to one point of a fluid in a closed container, the force is transmitted equally to all parts of the fluid.

periscope   A device that uses mirrors to allow you to see around corners and above your head.

persistence of vision   The process that causes your brain to see an image after it is no longer there because of the time lag between when you see an object and when the image registers in your brain.

pitch   The property of sound that makes it high or low.

point retinal image   An image whose reflected light is in focus at one point on the retina.

potential energy   Energy that is stored for later use.

proton   A positively charged subatomic particle found in the nucleus of an atom.

pulley   A simple machine made from a rope or cable that is looped around a wheel and that is used to change the amount or direction of a pulling force.

reflect   To bounce back.

repulsion   The electric or magnetic force that drives particles of matter apart.

resonance   The process of enriching a sound with supplementary vibrations.

rotor   The part that rotates in a motor or generator.

scientific method   A process used to investigate a problem. Involves making a hypothesis, testing it with an experiment, analyzing the results, and drawing a conclusion.

sound   The form of energy that lets us hear.

sound waves   Vibrations of sound energy that travel through the air.

stethoscope   A device that amplifies the sounds of the body such as a heartbeat.

stretch   To pull apart.

thaumatrope   A device that uses fast moving pictures to create a movie.

vision   The sense of the eyes that lets us see.

volt   A measure of the amount of energy an electric current carries.

volume   The amount of space an object occupies.

water pressure   The force exerted by water that has been compressed.

work   The transfer of energy by the force exerted on an object in order to move it.

Index

Made in the USA
Lexington, KY
19 December 2011